FALLING DARK

FALLING DARK

TIM THARP

MILKWEED EDITIONS

The characters and events in this book are fictitious. Any similarity to real persons, living or dead, is coincidental and not intended by the author.

© 1999, Text by Tim Tharp
All rights reserved. Except for brief quotations in critical articles or reviews, no part of this book may be reproduced in any manner without prior written permission from the publisher: Milkweed Editions, 1011 Washington Avenue South, Suite 300, Minneapolis, MN 55415. (800) 520-6455. www.milkweed.org

Published 1999 by Milkweed Editions
Printed in the United States
Cover design by Adrian Morgan, Red Letter Design
Cover photo by Photodisc
Interior design by Anja Welsh and Karin Simoneau
The text of this book is set in Janson.
01 02 03 04 05   5 4 3 2 1
First Paperback Edition

The Milkweed National Fiction Prize is underwritten in part by a grant from the Star Tribune Foundation.

Milkweed Editions, a nonprofit publisher, gratefully acknowledges additional support from the Elmer L. and Eleanor J. Andersen Foundation; James Ford Bell Foundation; Bush Foundation; General Mills Foundation; Honeywell Foundation; McKnight Foundation; Minnesota State Arts Board through an appropriation by the Minnesota State Legislature; Norwest Foundation on behalf of Norwest Bank Minnesota; Lawrence and Elizabeth Ann O'Shaughnessy Charitable Income Trust in honor of Lawrence M. O'Shaughnessy; Oswald Family Foundation; Ritz Foundation on behalf of Mr. and Mrs. E. J. Phelps Jr.; John and Beverly Rollwagen Fund of the Minneapolis Foundation; St. Paul Companies, Inc.; Star Tribune Foundation; Target Foundation on behalf of Dayton's, Mervyn's California, and Target Stores; U.S. Bancorp Piper Jaffray Foundation on behalf of U.S. Bancorp Piper Jaffray; and generous individuals.

Library of Congress Cataloging-in-Publication Data

Tharp, Tim, 1957–
    Falling dark / Tim Tharp. — 1st. ed.
        p.   cm.
    ISBN 1-57131-030-4 (cloth), 1-57131-034-7 (paper)
    I. Title.
    PS3570.H335F35   1999
    813'.54—dc21   99-18182
                                                                              CIP

This book is printed on acid-free paper.

Thanks to Maxine Tharp for giving me
some of her stubborn determination
and to Bill Tharp, Sr., whose voice
touches whatever I write.

FALLING DARK

None of the doors were locked. Ragel and all his brothers and sisters came and went, smiling and haphazard, and the front door itself stood open. Ragel said, Why should the doors be locked? My parents are home, and Nelson just shook his head. He knew doors had locks for a reason, but still Ragel walked out into the crisp air, leaving the front door open behind them. They walked around the side of the house and into the garage where Ragel's father worked at the massive wooden bench, a screwdriver clasped in one of his large brown hands, a strange scattering of what looked like clockwork laid out before him on the cork table-top. Nelson hadn't been to a black person's house before and he looked around now to discover whether there might be any sign of difference, of blackness, but could only think of how neat the place was: cardboard boxes taped and stacked in straight square towers, hammers and wrenches and garden spades hung snugly in rows from the pegboard wall, and lawn tools lined up like soldiers in the clean-swept corner, and so maybe that was something about black people, neatness and order and even the lawn mower clean.

The fishing tackle glinted in a green chest by the wall and the rods hung on hooks on the brown perforated board, their lines taut and secured, red-and-white plastic bobbers and lead sinkers and slyly grinning lures already strung. Mr. Daily lifted them down and into their hands, and looking up at him was like looking up the trunk of some deep-rooted tree. Strong brown hands and wide-chested and the smell of a pipe. And maybe that was black too: strength and neatness and unlocked doors.

On the other side of the road from Ragel's house lay a vacant lot and next to that a gutted house with burn marks black around the windows, tree limbs hanging over the bare ribs of the roof, the grass and weeds high and vines reaching up the stark, weathered edifice, a strangled and abandoned place. A place where pain must have been and cries and now everyone gone and Nelson had to look away. The sun was halfway down in the sky and it was fall and the woods were yellow and in some places orange and still green in places throughout. The road was a new blacktop, but they didn't take the road. Instead they cut through the tough yellow grass beside the burned-out house and it didn't matter how high the grass was or how stiff or thick or anything about cockleburs. They walked with their

4

arms raised, holding fishing poles above their heads as though wading through a high ocean surf. The air held a slight chill, and a flurry of birds burst from a near thicket and something else rustled away through the underbrush, frightened by the footsteps and voices, some scared thing in the hidden world.

The overgrown field let out onto a paved road and the road dipped and rose and at the peak the horizon circled, on one side a knife-edged plateau specked with gnarled trees and on the other a hill dotted with trailer houses buried in the foliage and then the edge of the campus at the technical college and its low, sloping athletic field feeling deep, like the cool cupped floor of a canyon, the fall sky above and hard bristled grass crunching underfoot. The pond lay beyond that, a small gray circle with two white swans and a gaggle of Canada geese and little goose turds curled in the crisp tendrils at the water's edge. The boys sat and unhooked their lines, looped them away into the near water, sending circles wafting outward and the flustered geese squawking away, their voices like rusty hinges, then nothing but the coolness rising from the water and a dank smell and sometimes smoke too, down in a wide place.

They watched their lines. It was cool and quiet. Nelson thought of Ragel's father and how his presence had filled every corner of the large garage and after a while he asked did his father ever take him swimming out at the lake and did they go up to the telephone company where he worked or to Tulsa to ride the roller coaster and Ragel said sure they did, they'd done all those things. Nelson nodded, watching his line. Was it pretty scary on that old roller coaster? he asked and at first Ragel said naw but then he said maybe a little and Nelson said he guessed that a lot of things were a little bit scary. My father was going to take me, he said. He was going to take me as soon as I got big enough. In the middle of the pond, a fish jumped and disappeared into rippling circles but no fish bit at the boys' lines.

Ragel said, You could go with me and my dad sometime, and Nelson nodded again, his eyes still on the water. A swan floated by, close but wary, its hard black eye surveying the fishermen. I want to go right up the top of one those roller coaster hills, Nelson said, staring at the swan. All the way up to where you can look off at everything, the whole countryside and all like that, and I'd take my hands off the bar and ride straight down the track all the way to the bottom of that hill, the biggest one, with my eyes wide open all the time and my hands up in the air the whole way down and not screaming or anything, just riding, and then come right up the other side. If I could do that, I wouldn't be scared anymore. I'd ride that old thing all day long.

In the hour they were there, they caught no fish and that didn't matter. It was an era all to itself with no need for souvenirs. When it had waned on its own they took up their gear, dusted their britches, and started back across the low field, down the hill and into the high grass. Ragel said his father would drive Nelson home but Nelson looked at the neat brick house with its close-cut lawn and green window trim and warm lights so different from where he lived now, a real family's house, and he said no, he would walk. It wasn't that far, he said, and he liked to walk when it was cool and the sun was going down.

So it was good-bye and Nelson hiked along the shoulder of the blacktop road, where the low-hanging limbs reached just above his head, and dodged into the street where the branches obstructed his way. The sky was deep blue and darkening and the chill sharpened. A quail rattled out of the grass and onto a low-slung fence wire. There was a sound of grinding gears somewhere and from somewhere still the crisp smell of wood smoke in the air. Nelson would have sung a song to himself if he could have thought of one and then he did think of one that his father used to sing but it had bad feelings to it now and there was no way to sing it anymore.

Behind him tires trundled on the blacktop and as the weathered truck rattled past he quickened his pace and veered farther from the shoulder into the knee-high grass and a thin twig whipped his shoulder and with his hand he cut a spider-web thread that slung down before him. Some fifty yards down the road, just past a narrow bridge, the truck suddenly swerved into the oncoming lane and then lurched to a halt along the grassy shoulder. Tree limbs brushed the cab top and the truck sat idling, a low growl and then a cough and then the growl again. Nelson stopped among the weeds watching, ducking slightly and leaning away, grabbing a low twig to steady himself. The way he had come offered no alternate route, no side streets or alleys, only the dense fields surrounding, and the truck still sat idling as two men, little more than silhouettes, one in a baseball cap, the other bareheaded, stepped out and walked around to the front. The truck idled and the dark figures leaned down out of view and the rusted tailgate hung open as though waiting for something. Shadows spread in the weeds and at the bottoms of the scrub oaks and the deep bruise blue of the sky spread and deepened. I'll just walk right on by, Nelson said to himself, they don't have anything to do with me and I'll just walk right on by. He pictured himself, hands in pockets, head turned straight, striding quickly and then past, but he didn't move from his place in the high brush.

Then beside him, the squeak of brakes and a car there, the old green Ford, breathing low and steady, his brother in their mother's car. I been looking for you, Wesley said.

Ragel told me you came down this way. The

window was rolled down and he squinted and brushed back his brown hair from his forehead. A slow song played on the radio, an old one by a woman who had fallen to pieces, and You should of been home already, Wesley said. Go on and get in.

Down the road the truck remained and sat idling as they passed, the windows dark, and in front the two men kneeling on the blacktop looking down at something, a small shadow, vague and shifting on the road before them.

Home was on the north side of town, where a gravel road gave way to countryside, scrub oaks and milkweed and sumac. A chain-link fence started by the gravel drive but soon sagged and sank and disappeared in the yellow grass, as limp as a vanquished flag. The wooden front porch sat swaybacked and on the chipped posts hung loose numbers, a nine and a six nearly reversed and a three swinging sideways. Shingles pried loose by wind and hail, chipped shutters hanging crooked, a gray, crumbling shelter in need of repair, waiting for the family that would do it and Nelson thought they were that family sometimes, he and his brother and their mother. But inside there was a deep feeling of silence and the lights were shut off and around the floor and on the tables lay splayed magazines and half-empty glasses and caked plates. Wesley picked them up as Nelson searched from empty room to empty room and then a note on the refrigerator: Spaghetti-Os in the cupboard and I'll be back around nine I'm with Maggie. And Nelson started to call out to Wesley but he knew Wesley knew and so stood silent looking across the sink and out the window where shadows lengthened in the yard and the far hills rose in the distance like the turned backs of grieving giants afraid to face the falling dark.

Maggie Daniels turned the car radio down and said, We won't stay too long, and Donna Bless said, I know that we won't, I've got two kids waiting at home and I've had to leave them to fix their own dinner while I'm at work enough as it is. It was bad enough at our old house, but I hate the thought of them rummaging around in that creaky rent house by theirselves all evening.

Well, you have to get out sometime too, Maggie said, or you'll go crazy. And it's not like you're gonna have some knight ride up on his horse and swoop you up with him, and Donna said she didn't expect something like that. That kind of thing only happened once. She looked out the window at the row of gray houses, and she could picture it clearly, Jack in his blue uniform stepping out of the power company truck. Jack walking toward her, smiling. Only he always used to say she was the one who swept him off his feet, and now the feelings from those times almost pushed through, like light through a heavy curtain.

You're in my town now, Maggie said. Here you have to go out and get what you want for yourself if you're gonna get anything. She looked back at the road and took one hand away from the steering wheel, flourishing her cigarette like a wand ready to invoke some magic incantation.

I guess, Donna said. But I think I must be about sixty watts short of having the same kind of energy you have for it. Even in the dimming light Maggie seemed almost to glow, her long red hair curling past her white shoulders, freckled cheeks and blue eyes sparked with a concentrated determination as though she were making up her mind to pry open the night and pull out everything she deserved.

Donna knew she didn't radiate brightness like that anymore or any determination at all. She was darker and more like ashes than sparks, her own eyes a walnut brown, her long hair straight and limp and almost as dark as her eyes, parted in the middle still, the same as it was the day she met Jack and the day she said good-bye to him too. She was short and these days bordering on wide through the hips, but not so different from how she had been in high school when her own fair number of boys came after her, a long way back in that other time.

What's this guy's name anyway? she asked.

Gary.

Gary. You can't tell much from that, can you?

The neighborhood didn't offer any more clues either. Large white houses with upstairs porches and gabled windows mixed with faded rent houses that seemed all but given up on and Donna pushed her hair away from her face and peered hard at the small clapboard house that Maggie turned toward, the dull wood facade behind a tangled hedge and dead flower stalks. It didn't look like a promising beginning for something new but she had told herself to stop thinking like that.

At the door they were met by a tall man with thinning brown hair and a walrus mustache half hiding his smile. He looked to be forty or so, a good ten years older than Maggie and a couple older than Donna herself. Maggie asked whether he ever intended to ask them inside, and he said sure he did, without looking anywhere but down toward her breasts. His name was Alex and he led them into the living room where they stood among the bare shadows and sparse furniture. His ex-wife got most of it in the divorce, he said, and Gary wasn't there yet. He had some trouble at work, Alex said, still staring straight into Maggie's white cleavage.

Did you lose something down in there? Donna asked him.

He finally raised his eyes. What's that?

Nothing, she said and he looked confused for a second and then went on about how Gary had to stay at the plant and straighten things out and they'd meet him for a few beers at a place called Checkers.

Donna said she didn't know about that. She didn't drink beer anymore or any kind of alcohol if he really wanted to know the truth and she had to be getting back early. Alex gave Maggie a look like, What is this specimen you've brought over here? and Maggie grabbed Donna's wrist and said, Oh, we have time for one beer at least. One little beer never did anybody any harm.

I don't know, Donna said. But she did know. She knew all about it.

In the near dusk the two men, one black-capped, shorter and wiry, the other younger, large and bareheaded, walked from the truck and down the dirt road, then veered into the bar ditch and up into the high grass. One orphan cloud hung low and gray and ragged on the far horizon and trees rose up around the perimeter of the field, stark, almost naked. Still neither man spoke. The tall one, Charlie, shambled among the dry stalks, and Roy Dale carried a burlap sack first dangling from one fist then switching and they traversed the pasture and entered the dark line of trees and settled in a clearing where the red ice chest and rusted lawn chairs sat beside the makings of a campfire, a gathering of limbs as bare and dry as a stack of bones.

Get the lighter fluid out of my backpack over

there, Roy said. He sat in a lawn chair and tipped the baseball cap back on his head. I'll get the hot links and the buns done up. The bigger one hunkered over the canvas backpack by the ice chest and drew out the tin can and sprayed a generous amount over the wood and lit it, his face breaking into a grin as the initial burst of flames jumped up.

Don't get that sonofabitch too bright, Roy said. I don't want Sam coming out here accusing us of anything again.

Charlie stared back into the fire, a look of vague concern replacing the smile. The timber crackled and light flickered on the tree trunks and it was almost like being inside of a cave in some ancient world. Roy drew out a pint bottle of whiskey and took a long pull and offered it to his partner and the two of them traded drinks, sitting in their decayed lawn chairs, boots kicked out in front of them and the heat from the fire on their faces, the burlap sack lying limp on the forest floor between them.

What're we going to do with this old thing here, Roy? Charlie said, nudging the sack with his foot. Roy looked down and the fire lit one side of his face and he kicked the sack hard. I figured we'd give it to Sam for his birthday, he said. We'll put him a cigarette in his mouth and stick a beer can up under his hand and set him out on Sam's porch. I can just see his face when he comes out and takes a look at that.

Charlie looked thoughtful for a second, then said, You think we could barbecue him? and Roy raised his eyebrows. Hell no, Charlie, you want to make yourself sick? Charlie looked at the fire and didn't say anything. From his seat he sprayed another loop of fluid into the flames and they jumped again and he smiled, more sedately this time. Maybe we can make us some hats out of it, he said then. I bet it'd make a dynamite hat, and Roy said, Maybe. He lit a marijuana cigarette and inhaled deeply, then passed it to Charlie and the strong smell of it hung in the air.

Between them the burlap sack moved. Charlie flinched and the cigarette dropped to the ground. Did you see that? he said, cautiously picking up the cigarette. Did you see that sonofabitch move? Roy said he didn't see any such thing. He said it couldn't have moved because they'd killed it already. Charlie shook his head and inhaled from the cigarette, a worried look in his eye as he watched the sack, and it moved again.

There it went, Charlie said, wriggling in his seat. There it went again.

Well, I'll be damned, Roy said. I saw the fucker that time. But it isn't gonna move for long. He kicked the sack hard again and then another time but it rustled and squirmed and emitted a hoarse angry hissing and Charlie kicked it, tentatively at first then harder, but the sack only squirmed more violently. Stop kicking it a minute, Roy said, I got an idea. Just back off for a second. And they both backed off and the sack settled down. Roy drew a bone-handled knife from his pants pocket and folded out the blade and knelt down and cut a six-inch slit along the top of the sack. It squirmed again and a small black hand reached out of the hole and clawed the air then withdrew and was replaced by a dark narrow snout and then the whole masked face squeezed through. The raccoon peered fretfully at the fire and then at Roy and then at the woods beyond.

He's gonna get away, Charlie said, almost panicking, but Roy said it wouldn't get loose if he had anything to do about it. He wasn't going to let any raccoon make a fool out of him and he pulled a bare white limb from the fire, one end of it glowing orange. I'm gonna conduct a little experiment, he said and waved the stick toward the raccoon's face and it flinched and hissed and struggled in its bondage. Charlie laughed. Do it again, do it again, and Roy tapped the glowing end of the stick against the raccoon's snout. It rolled away onto its side, fighting against the burlap, and Roy poked at its snout and it bleated in pain and smoke rose from the fur.

Leaping awkwardly, Charlie grabbed up his own limb from the fire and with its end still flaming jabbed the sack, singeing a black mark into it, then through. The animal tried to roll away but Roy jumped to the other side and they took turns with their burning

16

pokers. The raccoon tried to pull its head in but was caught, one black hand snared between his snout and the burlap, and he could only bare his teeth in an almost comical grimace and he wriggled and lunged and hissed but the sticks kept coming. That little sonofabitch is fried out, Charlie said and laughed and slashed his stick through the air like a sword-fighter's blade. Look out, I'll get him on the nose again, get out of the way, Roy said and took aim but hit the eye and the raccoon shrieked in an almost human voice. Charlie laughed and dropped his stick and kept laughing. Damn he's pissed now, Roy said and dust rose where the animal struggled and the smell of burning hair and fierce cries in the air and the two men working around the sack in a primitive dance.

Then in the middle of it a voice called out from the edge of the clearing and their legs froze and the churning arms left off their frantic motion. What the hell's going on down in here? The voice was closer and they knew it was Sam. Charlie quit laughing and Roy held the poker down by his side and neither answered as the tall man walked into the firelight, broad shoul-dered, a massive forehead, bald with long graying hair on the sides curling over his ears. The reflection of the fire flickered on the strong lines of his jaw and in his angry eyes and Let that damn animal alone, he said, his gaze fixed on the writhing sack.

We was just having us a little sport there, boss,

17

Roy said, backing away, and Charlie said, That's right, Sam, that's all we was doing.

When Sam stepped forward, Roy stood in front of him for a second, his arms crossed on his chest, but he thought better of it and retreated to the rusted lawn chair and Sam kneeled beside the sack, his large frame blocking the raccoon from view, and Jesus, Jesus, he said and then it was loose and springing away from the clearing, a shadow sucked back into the dark. My God, Sam said, haven't you sorry assholes got anything better to do? Why don't you go on into town and give my place a rest for a change?

Roy looked at Charlie and Charlie stared away into the fire and the trees circled in a black cup around them. Hell, Roy said, it was just a little sport.

The beer sign was a sort of bleeding red neon and Donna stared into it, avoiding even a glance at the open bottles around the bar, focusing all her attention on that red haze, a color she knew well from all her late-night drinking sprees, redness the color of a deep-cut sorrow beating in the dark. That was the way she would have seen it then. An eternal sorrow, the sorrow of the heart of God and she had known it fully and was part of it, inside of it. That was what drinking had been after all, not drowning pain or running from it, like those people at the DUI classes told you to believe, but entering into pain whole, living inside of it, and only drunk had she been able to feel anything for so long that all her life before seemed to have taken place on the other side of a gaping canyon and now that she was trying to stay sober she could only see it in the distance, like pantomime figures waving their arms into the air.

But still she could see it. The girl in grade school everyone was afraid to dare because they knew she would take it up. The girl in the red Camaro. The bride who got married at the Pawnee Bill Wild West Ranch and Museum. The wife who made love to her husband one night on the roof of the house, holding on with one hand to the TV antenna. The mother who invented games for her boys and taught them how to dance standing on the tops of her shoes, the Rolling Stones playing on the stereo. Jumping Jack Flash and Wild Horses and Time Is on My Side.

Next to her, Gary said, What? and she realized she'd said something out loud. He sat on the stool, his elbows splayed on the bar top, his wide red face leaned toward her. It was the mysteries of reupholstery and his vintage Impala he had been going on and on about and now his eyes squinted up over being interrupted.

Nothing, she said. I just never met anyone who knew so much about upholstery.

We could go out and take a look at it if you want.

That's all right.

You sure you don't want a beer? he asked. Might loosen you up some. His expression twisted into what must have been meant to hint at some kind of conspiracy of desire but she was far removed from anything like that at the moment.

Me and beer don't get along, she said. Or maybe we just got along too good.

He shook his head over that and ordered his own beer, then mumbled something about how she ought to try getting along with the case of Coronas he had on ice at his house. His thick hair was stiff and heavily sprayed and his beard flecked with gray and who did he think he was anyway, Donna wanted to know, Wolfman Jack or somebody. But he wasn't any Wolfman Jack, he was shift supervisor at Stuart Glass and divorced, all in the red beer sign glow, and if there was anything more sad than him in the world, Donna didn't know what it was. But oh yes she did. Oh yes she did.

On her other side Maggie collapsed onto a bar stool and fanned her face with her hand to cool off from dancing and Alex stood grinning so wide that his mustache spread out like a thing ready to take flight. My God, woman, aren't you ever going to get off that bar stool? Maggie said and Donna just smiled.

So what do you think of Gary? Maggie whispered, leaning in close.

Well, I guess if I ever need anything reupholstered I'll know who to call anyway.

Maggie laughed and said, I thought mine's mustache was bad but come on, look at that beard why

20

don't you. And then the taped music started again and Alex pulling her away and they glided onto the small dance floor where the colored lights spun on their clothes.

Donna was still watching them when Gary's hand clamped hard on her arm and him tugging her, saying, No use putting it off any longer, if you're not ready now you never will be, and she let herself be led and then pulled into his arms. She had never liked this kind of country music but it was easy anyway to melt into the melody and weave among the other dancers, Gary's meaty chest pressed so close she felt nearly smothered and his cologne an atmosphere all its own. He tried to twirl her but she wasn't expecting it and nearly fell and he pulled her back laughing, his beard in her hair, his cracked lips on her neck and some vague murmur just out of earshot. Then she felt it on her abdomen, him already hard against her, and she thought of several jokes about it but they were all too sad to tell.

The pickup truck shook across the buckled road and Roy Dale thumbed his crumbling cigarette out the window, sending sparks trailing into the dark. How about we go to that one place we always use to like, Charlie said, and Roy looked at him.

What place are you talking about now?

You know that place with the naked women on bicycles up in the bathroom.

21

Hell, Roy said, that place's for losers. Pass me up a cold one. Charlie withdrew a beer bottle from the small ice chest on the floorboard and handed it to Roy. The lights of town glowed in the distance and along the roadside now little crooked stores and the auto salvage, a barbecue restaurant and beyond that teenagers' cars parked in a circle outside the Git-N-Go. Would you look at that little high-school pussy, Roy said, craning his neck as they passed. Standing beside a black Trans Am a blond girl shook back her hair and cocked her hand on her jutted hip. I tell you what, I'd bang that stuff now, Roy said, and Charlie whistled and without even looking out the window said, Hot damn, man, that's some dynamite pussy.

Roy took a drink of beer and wiped his hand across his mouth, letting the truck steer itself for a second before grabbing back onto the wheel. Looking at the stoplight ahead, he squinted and said, You know what, that damn Sam can go to hell. What's he doing getting all self-righteous about a fucking old coon anyway? That's what I want to know. Telling us what to do on our own damn time. He better watch his ass, that's all I can say.

Charlie cocked his head to the side. Aw, Sam's all right.

Just because a bastard gives you a paycheck doesn't make him all right, Roy said. You know he's got a bunch more money out there than we'll ever see, don't you? You ever see that sonofabitch hardly ever buy anything? Naw, he's got a good-size chunk stashed around there.

That's all right, Charlie said. I don't care how much money he has.

Roy stared at the road and After all I been through with Sam, he said, I'll be damned if he's going to start acting like my old man on me or something. He does, he better damn well watch out, I'll slap his ass right down like I did my old man too. Shit. I ever tell you about that?

You told me about that plenty of times.

That old bastard better be glad he run off. All the shit he did to me. I should of slapped his ass till he couldn't get back up again. By God. Sam doesn't know who he's dealing with if he doesn't think I'll be all over his ass too the next time he tries to talk to me that way.

I like that place with the little pool tables, Charlie said. They got a dynamite jukebox.

Roy clenched the steering wheel tight with one hand and said, I told you, forget that place. He said, I want to look at some real women tonight, not some pictures of a bunch of skank on bicycles on the wall. And quit saying dynamite so much, why don't you. It gets on my nerves.

Donna said she was tired of dancing and why didn't they just call it a night but Gary wasn't quite ready for that. In the parking lot behind the bar, he pressed her against the fender of the vintage Chevrolet Impala. Dancing always gives me a lot of energy, he said. A lot of energy.

I'm worn out, she said and tried to turn away.

It's still early, he said, pressing close, his hands clamped to her arms. I'm just getting cranked up.

I have to get home to my boys, she said and leaning his face closer he told her, Just a little while longer, and then his mouth down over hers, the taste of cigarette breath and his beard scouring her face, and Baby, baby, he said like some old song from the sixties. We're just getting started, he said, one hand moving under her blouse, hot on her stomach, the other stroking her thigh and she said, Hold on there Valentino, just hold on, but she wasn't sure if he heard it with all his heavy breathing and halting groans and then his pants undone and him naked and hard against her, both his hands digging into her from behind now, pulling her upward and him lunging. Oh baby.

Hey now, she said louder. Hey now, you just quit that stuff. She pushed his chest but he pressed over her and had leverage and weight. She started to holler but he planted his mouth over hers, rough and smoky, and she wriggled and suddenly lost her balance, falling hard to the parking lot, him on top of her laughing. You are the crazy one. I like that, I like that wild stuff now. You like that wild stuff, baby? You like that wild stuff? His body pressing heavy, his face lowering, wide and swollen and framed by sprayed hair gone wild and his hand pushing between her thighs. We're gonna get real wild.

Then suddenly he reeled backward, a great relief of pressure from her chest, and the stars circling around, wheeling above, and a man with a black baseball cap, mustache and lean face hovering there too, You're gonna get you some wild stuff all right, you sonofabitch. By God you're gonna get all you can handle.

Gary cocked sideways on the parking lot, his face quizzical for a second and then his head snapped back as the boot kicked his chin and he sprawled onto his back and the man with the hat kicked him in the side of the face. Donna teetered to her knees and Oh God, she said. Oh God. And the man straddled Gary and slapped him in the face over and over, steadily, methodically, a high-arching swing until his hand was bloody and he finally stopped and rocked back. Hadn't you got anything better to do than pick on some little girl out here? he said, Gary limp and bloody beneath him, his swollen lips stammering some half-finished plea.

Donna struggled to stand but lost her balance again and sank back to the pavement and then the man there grabbing her, his cap knocking against her forehead and falling to the ground and Whoa there, he said. It's okay, I got you. The whole world spinning end over end and sideways too and Gary only a few feet away, struggling to drag his pants up over his pasty white thighs.

It's gonna be all right, the man holding her said. You're gonna be just fine, and replacing his cap, he turned to Gary, his voice changing to a harsh tone now, Get those damn britches up and get the hell out of here.

Still fumbling at his zipper, Gary stumbled away to the Impala and rattled his keys into the door lock. The headlights spread out on the pavement and the engine turned over and when the man with the cap stood, the car backed away.

Donna sat back on the pavement and looked at him, his brown eyes and lean jaw and hawk nose. And just next to him a younger man, an overgrown kid really, somewhere in his early twenties, with thick lips and small eyes. Can you stand up all right? the first man said, kneeling back down and putting his arms around her. She said that she guessed she could. She was just a little bit in shock was all and she was sure glad he came along like he did. He smiled at her and his eyes sharpened and he said, So am I. He turned to the big man beside him and Get a beer out of the truck for the lady, why don't you Charlie. I think she could use one right about now.

That's all right, she said. I just need to get out of here, that's all. I just need to go home.

Don't you worry, we got plenty to spare. A whole

ice chest full. He helped her stand and walked her toward a pickup truck with the door hanging open. His
friend pulled back from the door, a dark brown bottle
in his hand, bits of ice and streaks of water sliding
down the glass. They're nice and cold, he said, holding
the bottle out to her.

Well, okay, she told him. Thanks. I guess I could
use something to wash this taste out of my mouth. But
then I have to be getting home.

It was the dream and even inside it Nelson knew it was
the dream and what would come but knowing didn't
take away from the dream's power and even made him
feel that much more trapped within the murky process
of it. There were the three teenagers all alike, their
stringy oily hair cut straight in front and hiding their
eyes, white nylon jackets and ripped jeans, holes and
holes all over their clothes and ragged white tennis
shoes. They walked through the wall just like appari-
tions and he ran into the dark woods and they came
down from the trees, dropped straight in front of him
and never spoke but stood with their hands in their
jacket pockets and he knew what they had there, he
knew and couldn't do anything about it and he ran and
was on his old street in the old neighborhood with the
shining cars in the driveways and the clean porches
and polished-looking brick, people on their fresh-cut
lawns smiling under the moon, smiling and nodding

and Why are you running Nelson, why are you running? There's no one behind you. And he knew the teenagers weren't behind him now, they were in front, they were on the yard of his own house, they were on the driveway where his father's truck from the power plant sat and then stepping onto the porch and he ran and they were ringing the doorbell and he called out, Don't answer it Daddy, don't answer, don't answer, but there they stood under the porch light, their backs turned, their hands withdrawing from their pockets and the door opening before them and Nelson hollered and hollered but it didn't do any good. It never did. His father stood in the wan light smiling and it was too late and Nelson awoke.

In the dark of the bedroom, shapes emerged, the faint white of the curtains and the lamp like a head in the corner and the mingled figures in the open closet and he tried to think the good thoughts, the thoughts of the earliest, earliest days. In the lake in summer, the whole world green and blue and his father holding him around the middle, telling him to paddle and stroke and There you are, that's the man, that's the little man. Holding him around the middle and Nelson could never sink or fail or be swept away. And the roller coaster too, the whole track trembling as the cars rumbled past, the rush of the air at the curve, the children crying out and the high hill where the car looked as though it would fly into the trees. He wanted to ride and he wouldn't be scared, he said. And he wouldn't have been either, not with his father there. But his father said no, he was too small. See the sign, his father said, you have to be taller than the clown's hand, and Nelson stared at the clown as though he were a sworn enemy then and his father said, That's all right, we'll ride it another time. We'll ride it another time.

The memory fell on him then, crashing, an avalanche of shattered black glass, the stories of the teenagers witnessed that night in the stolen Cutlass and he always knew what they looked like even though nobody else really did, the teenagers waiting in the shadows with torn tennis shoes and a homemade gun. The doorbell ringing over and over. Don't answer it Daddy, don't answer it this time. Then the shot, just a frail popping, like a dropped book or a snapped branch, and he comes to the edge of the living room and sees his mother over him with blood on the white shirt she slept in. The white shirt with the teddy bear on front. How could there be blood on that? And her hand raised to her face, red, and blood on her cheek. Her mouth open and some sound that couldn't even be called a voice starting from somewhere inside her.

Then Wesley sitting on the car bumper the night after the funeral with all the adults inside and ham on the table and in the refrigerator and ham everywhere. Why did they do it? Nelson asked. Why did they have to go and do something like that? Over and over he asked that question. For three days he asked it and Wesley answered sharply finally without ever turning, Quit asking me that, just quit asking me that. I don't know why they did it. They didn't have to have a reason. They just did it. They just walked up and did it as easy as ringing the bell.

The tears burned hot trails on Nelson's cheeks. He tried not to cry but he did and Wesley looked at him then and put his hand on his shoulder and said it was all right to cry about it and his words were softer. There isn't always a reason for things, he said. Sometimes things just happen.

Wesley said something else too and Nelson couldn't remember whether he said it that night or later but he remembered the narrowed look in his eyes, almost like an old man's eyes. I'm going to track those guys down, Wesley said, I'm going to track those guys down and kill them deader than all the ghosts in hell. And nobody's ever going to come in and hurt anyone I know ever again. Don't you worry, just don't you worry.

Nelson thought those words over and over now in bed until the sound of a slamming car door outside broke them. He pulled up the red blanket and wrapped it around him and walked to the window. On the chest of drawers against the wall the little cowboy clock said it was almost two-thirty and he knew what it meant when she came home late like that. There was a pickup truck in the grass, not even on the gravel but right in the grass and he could have sworn it was the same one he'd seen on the side of the road with the tailgate down. She laughed but he couldn't see her at first and then she was there, stumbling in the yard, reeling backward and then sideways and she tipped and teetered and spilled into the dried shrub by the burned-out lamp, laughing. A man was there too, a lean and hard man in a black baseball cap and faded leather coat, jeans and boots, and he wavered after her and stooped to help her up and almost fell himself. He spoke but the words were muffled. He pulled again and then she was up and falling forward into his chest and he held her against him and bowed his head into her long brown hair.

Then Wesley was there in nothing but an old pair of jeans. Mama, he said. Nelson heard him clearly. Mama, what are you doing? She pulled away from the man then and reached out her hand toward Wesley, a dreamy smile parting her face, her hair pasted to her cheek. Wesley went to her and grabbed her by one arm and he and the man helped her along for a second until Wesley turned to him and said something and then she said something too. The man said something back but still he halted and let go of her. She and Wesley continued on, her leaning heavily on his shoulder and then out of view and just the man left, standing alone, wavering, as though he might tumble backward at any time into the pale wash of moonlight on the dying grass behind him.

Sam Casey set the metal bucket next to the quail pen and walked along the rutted dirt trail watching the dawn split over the treetops. There was a slight mist in the trees and even over their highest branches and the sun coming up very orange above it. The sky would be a piercing blue today and Sam Casey felt very deep inside of himself, down through his forty-six years, for the stirrings of feelings as ancient as the childhood of all things, a connection to the umber fields stretching to the bony tree line and the gnarled scrub oaks and tattered green cottonwoods and wild thistle gone brown with the mechanics of October and to the mist itself moving like a spirit in the vague forest, like the spirit of the Grandfathers the Indians spoke of: Grandfather we come, we come to your place of flowering, we reap and we gather, Grandfather and the Great Spirit that moves through the rocks and the sacred stalks and our hearts, hear this soul and know it is grateful.

He stopped at the edge of the field. The feeling

had come and he walked back toward the house, the twisted oak out front where the tire swing had once hung for Melinda, and beyond that the weathered two-story farmhouse, a pioneer house, there since even before statehood, cracked white posts on the porch and wide windows, the humpbacked wood barn to the right and rear, door closed tight, crumbling, no doubt, but still structurally sound, good into the next millennium, and the house even stronger than that and all the land around standing guard.

The mist began to burn away, the sun climbing, yes, a piercing blue sky today and only the slightest chill in the air and best of all the sound of rattling skillets from the kitchen window and as soon as he stepped inside the smell of bacon frying. And surrounded by the clutter of utensils and ingredients, Melinda moved to the toaster with her box of frozen waffles, her strawberry blond hair soft on her shoulders. So are you about ready for breakfast? she asked without looking up and he told her he was.

You know, she said, if you'd find someone to get married to, you wouldn't have to wait for me to come out here and make it for you in the morning.

I wouldn't have it any other way, he said and she smiled, her straight and slender body tilting against the green counter, the sun on her face, her beige brocaded sweater now curving with small breasts he could barely acknowledge. He looked instead at her lighted face,

33

peacefully smiling over her work, her expression almost as it had been at twelve or ten, the little Irish-girl face, nose, eyes, and mouth collected close together, freckles and long, nearly translucent eyelashes closing softly over the pale blue eyes with every compliment paid her. And he would never mention real waffles the way he used to make them for her when she was a girl or the bitterness of the coffee because she was here. She was here and the coffee could taste like turpentine and waffles be hard as manhole covers and still nothing could be as sweet.

When the breakfast was ready they sat at the Formica-topped table, she straight across, her face tilted shyly down, her pale blue eyes looking upward through the light eyelashes and he could have stared at her never saying a word but he knew it made her uneasy so he talked about the quail and how he almost hated to sell them but there was no way around it, a man had to make a living and maybe it wasn't much of a living but it sure beat the slow nine-to-five death that most people called a living. But he was going on too much and stopped.

She smiled and chipped at her waffle with the tip of her fork and said, I think Mama thinks you're doing something illegal up here. I heard her talking to Dan about it and I came in the room and they stopped talking.

Sam stared hard into his coffee. It was light with

cream and a wisp of steam trailing up and he told her
that her mother only said things like that because she
was married to a cop. But Dan isn't a cop, Melinda
said, he's a history teacher at the technical college, and
Sam took a drink of the coffee, set it down and said
that it didn't matter because people out there most of
them had the hearts of cops whether they actually
were cops or not and especially history teachers.

I don't, she said, and I live out there. He looked
at her then and said, Oh no, I know you don't but you
got the inoculation, and he smiled.

Besides, she said, Dan couldn't ever be a cop because all he does is come home from work and drink
his scotch until he falls asleep on the couch.

That's what cops do too, Sam said but he wished
he hadn't and he wished he hadn't said anything at all
about the world out there because he didn't want to talk
about that or the round-shouldered history teacher
and he especially didn't want to talk about Melinda's
mother, who had once been part of his own inner dimensions and still was if he had to be truthful about it,
he only wanted to have his daughter here with him in
the old house in the heart of the woods. So he fell
quiet until she brought up high school and he listened
to her talk about her friends and how it was different
now that they were in high school and not junior high
and he resisted the temptation to ask her about her
history class or her government class because he knew

it would only lead him to castigate her teachers for passing off their imaginary fables as facts.

She wasn't worried about classes or teachers anyway, it was boys that she was thinking about now and he wasn't sure he was ready to hear her talk about a subject like that. Sometime he would be but not right now. The problem wasn't her own though, it was her friend Jennifer and the way she went with too many boys all the time for the wrong reasons.

I don't know about that girl, Sam said. I never did see why you ran around with her.

She's my friend, Melinda said, and he let it stay at that.

He finished his waffles and pushed back the plate and the room was full of sun now and it glinted off the copper rooster clock on the wall. She cut off a piece of waffle and swirled it in a thick pool of syrup and that reminded her, she said. She had been at the Dairy Queen and he'd never guess who she saw. She saw Roy Dale. He came up behind her and she almost dropped her strawberry sundae.

Sam set his coffee cup down and looked across the table. She would do best to keep her distance from Roy Dale, he told her. Roy Dale could be trouble if you gave him half a chance, and she asked him why he had anything to do with him then and he said, It's a long story but let's just say I owe him one.

In his mother's room the clock radio blared its tinny song, going on and on all about I'm Henry the Eighth I am I am and not shutting up until Wesley finally went in and turned it off. Come on, he told her, gently tugging loose the blue covers and she rolled away toward the wall. Come on, you have to get up. You know you don't want to lose any more jobs, and he pulled on her arm and helped her sit up though she barely looked awake and slouched there with eyes still shut, hair tangled and stuck to her cheek, sour with beer, her mouth opening and closing as though trying to forge words after a long time in exile. Finally she was able to stand and with the weight of her heavy against him he led her down the hall to the bathroom and stood until the shower sounded and then he went to the kitchen and put on the coffee.

When she came in and sat at the kitchen table, her face drawn and white, her long hair wet and the circles under her eyes, he set down her bowl of cereal and then the toast and she stared into the cereal for a long time. He thought she was trying not to cry and went to the window and looked out and didn't say anything. I should be making your breakfast, she said after a while and he said that it didn't matter, he didn't mind, and kept looking out the window. The sun shone bright on the chain-link fence and the sky was as blue as cold water. He wondered if she could notice such things now, the beauty of the little things, and he wished that instead of work he could take her out to the woods to some small and glassy lake where they would hike until the alcohol evaporated from her blood and then they would just sit there on a boulder or grassy hill, not even having to talk much but sitting and looking at the sky and the sun on the water and everything would be cleaned out.

The farmhouse slouched on its flat earth was always home but still seemed depleted somehow without her. Sam felt it again when he returned from taking her back to her mother's and no new substance was added by Charlie's presence on the front porch. He asked Charlie where Roy Dale was and Charlie said he was still in bed. He got home no telling how late and now he wouldn't get up for anything and just lay in bed with the pillow over his head moaning. Maybe if we wait, Charlie said, he'll still come later. Sam looked across the field and shook his head and said that later would be too late.

He fetched his backpack from the house and they set off on foot across the uneven field and entered the woods and continued down a narrow path lined by dried leaves and wiry tangles of obdurate brambles and high stalks almost as hard as cane. The sunlight came through in shafts and splintered on the low-hanging branches and spilled into pools in the sink-holes and gullies. Sam walked in front and Charlie

38

lumbered behind and they didn't talk for almost all of the hour-long hike. Finally, the trees gave way to a tilted creek bank and they crossed the creek by way of a felled trunk, its bark crackled and rotten and soggy, and then forged up the steeper bank on the far side and over.

At the crest of the hill they waded the near waist-high bluestem and in the bottom land before them stretching all the way to the far tree line rose a formidable jungle of tough weeds, thistle and blood-weed, spindle tree and poke, the ragged tangles reaching nearly sixteen feet tall in places and yellow, purple, and green and more green and something near crimson, an impenetrable wasteland for anyone who didn't see it as Sam did.

Whoo boy, Charlie said and Sam said, Yeah, and he led the way into the jungle, parting stiff foliage with his arms, following the faintest trace of a path, no more than a bending of ragged fronds in a certain direction, struggling forward until in front of them, barely distinguishable from the bloodweed, a tight cluster of four marijuana plants rising as tall as any other, their stalks the circumference of young trees, waving gracefully and rustling a quiet song, as innocent as some primitive tribe never touched by a civilized people.

Silently he inspected their color and size and scent, bending down one of the smaller plants and fingering the leaves of the kola gently, then surveying for the spot where the tarp would be placed and thinking of the hundreds of other plants hidden throughout the overgrown field and all the detailed logistics of the harvest and hauling away.

These ones over here are something else, Charlie called from somewhere in the weeds. They look all ripe for the taking, Sam. And Sam was quiet and respectful for a moment. We ought to wait for a good cold snap first, he said then. But next weekend should be about right.

Dynamite, Charlie said.

Sam worked his way back to the crest of the creek bank and contemplated the bottom land, a gnarled patch of summer in the middle of autumn and a thousand plants hidden among it, all full and healthy and the sky a piercing blue over them, a peaceful world, and he waited for the deep feeling inside and for a second thought it was coming, breaking through like a green seedling in a parched land, but he kept waiting and it didn't come.

That afternoon Wesley had his own job to go to and on the way Nelson rode with him. He knew Nelson wanted to ask about last night and the man and their mother but there were no answers to that so instead they talked about football. Nelson was all for the Dallas Cowboys being the team this year and Aikman and Irvin and Smith, now they were tough, nothing could get them down, and Aikman from right down south in Henryetta. And Wesley said sure Dallas was tough all right but this might be the year for the Packers, and then he looked at Nelson, small and almost frail in the seat beside him, and he had to agree Nelson might be right, Dallas was sure going to be strong, and things felt all right then and all that waited in the dark behind their words would stay there, staved back for a little while at least.

You should of gone out for football this year, Nelson said, and Wesley told him he couldn't because of work, and I sure wish you could though, Nelson said. I bet you would of been quarterback of the whole team. I bet you'd take over for Aikman someday down in Dallas if you got the chance, and Wesley smiled and said he didn't know about that and they looked at each other, both smiling.

They picked up Ragel on the way and Wesley drove them to a small park where the other boys from school waited to start the touch football game. Scrub oaks and maples and some firs dotted the park and on one side a steep hill rose up, studded with outcroppings of gray rock. The other boys in their colored sweat-shirts and ripped jeans mingled near a little rock pavilion and Wesley thought they looked a lot bigger than his brother. As they parked Nelson stared out the window and it appeared as though he might have been thinking they seemed pretty big too. He was short for his age and pale and stayed inside too much anymore and although he watched sports on the television set he never played as much as Wesley had when he was younger and maybe it wasn't even the idea of physical harm as much as the threat of some new hurt inside when healing already came so hard as it was.

Do you know these guys? Wesley asked, looking into the backseat at Ragel and Ragel said they were just some of the guys from school and he played football with them all the time. Uh-huh, Wesley said and looked at Nelson. Are you sure you want to play? I mean, it's been a while since you played any football, and Nelson stared toward the field, the faint traces of worry around the rims of his eyes, and he said, I'm sure.

Wesley glanced back at Ragel again and he seemed to understand and Wesley was grateful because there was no way to say any more out loud. Then Nelson and Ragel were out of the car, Ragel short-haired and almost pudgy and bouncing along while Nelson lagged behind just a little, his soft brown hair poking up on top, the handed-down sweatshirt so big on him he appeared to have almost no substance at all within it and if a hard wind bore down it would take him flying over the trees and away into the sky.

She survived the afternoon but evening came and the hangover wouldn't release her, everything muffled and foreign, a dimension of gray radio waves or some such strangeness ready to collapse inward at any moment, drawing her into a void of her own making and she knew it was all her own fault, nobody's but hers. Last week she had agreed to work overtime today and regretted it now, though she needed the money, and by seven her shoulders clutched and her head seemed to expand and contract, the pain in her back burning, her hands barely moving where they were told. The lines at her register seemed endless and all along the black conveyor belt it was rows of cat food and diapers and liter bottles of Coca-Cola as heavy and awkward as babies, bread and El Charrito Mexican dinners, shaving cream, Maalox, apples, Count Chocula and lettuce and lunch meat with olives embedded in it like little eyes looking at you and it was enough to turn your stomach some of the things people bought to eat and on top of that it was no ordinary grocery but a superstore that also sold blankets and wastebaskets and even chairs and cheap lamps and she dropped a cake and cracked an egg and a mirror fell over but at least didn't break. Once she felt dizzy and had to stand back and steady herself and the middle-aged woman there said, Honey are you all right? and she said that she was though she didn't believe it herself. Then a case of beer flowed down the conveyor belt and she couldn't bring herself to look at it and turned to the register, avoiding eye contact with the customer, as she had all day, but he said her name. The voice was strange, and the face at first didn't make sense, but it was him.

He smiled and raised his eyebrows and You're sure looking good, he said, and all the things from last night that she never wanted to think about again flooded back and looking at him now, his long black hair from under the black cap and the hard lines, hawk nose and mustache, she didn't know what she had been thinking but of course she hadn't been thinking, had she, and after all had been with worse than him some nights during that stretch when the rum and Coke took hold and wouldn't let go. But she had told herself never again and then what was his name at the club last night? Gary? Him straddling her on the hard parking lot with his trousers pulled down. But why did she end up on her back in that pickup truck then, the tattered seat covers sticking to her naked skin and this other one rocking on top of her, she didn't even know how they got there, but still felt his rough face on her chest like a burn, the stab and convulsions, the last collapsing breath, and it didn't make sense at all to do that, to fight off the one only to end up with this other one, all for that brief moment, the surge of liquid electricity inside, a few seconds that crumbled apart the same way every time.

Before her the conveyor belt wavered and buckled and she thought she might crash forward into it but steeled herself and he said, I got a case of beer I thought you might want to help me out with when you get off.

I'm going home when I get off, she told him, looking away at the shopping cart behind him. I'm going home and going to sleep for about twenty years.

Come on, he said with an exaggerated pleading tone and she didn't say anything but turned to the register, rang up the beer and told him the price. How about this, he said, how about just a couple of beers and maybe a game of pool somewhere, I got a whole bunch of money that just about wants to jump right out of my pocket, but she said she couldn't and told him the price again. Behind him the woman with the blue, blue eye shadow and the loaded shopping cart coughed. He withdrew his wallet and thumbed through slowly, the wide flat ends of his fingers moving with frustrating deliberation over the rumpled bills, and the woman coughed again and he looked at her and said, Hold your horses Grandma, this isn't a race. Then he turned back and said, Can you break a hundred, and she said that she could but he ended up giving her a twenty, making her pull on it twice before letting go. He smiled. I sure would like to take another ride out by the lake.

She made change and counted it out in his hand and when she was done he held onto her fingertips and said, Did anybody ever tell you you got eyes like a doe? Big old sad doe eyes. And she looked down at their hands and all of a sudden felt like screaming or crying, she wasn't sure which. Look, she said, straining to keep an even tone. I'm at work. I can't talk right now.

Leave, he said and she said, What? and looked at his face now, a grinning stranger who thought he knew something about her.

Just leave. Just walk right on out the front door with me right now and say to hell with it. Behind him the woman rattled her shopping cart back and steered it to another row. Donna pulled her hand away then and told him, You better go on now before you get me in trouble.

To hell with this place, he said, and she told him, Look, I got two boys and one already has to work almost forty hours a week and go to high school both. I can't lose this job. So I appreciate you helping me out last night but that doesn't mean we're going to go riding off into the sunset together, okay? Her voice shaking so that even he could see she was ready to break down and held out his hands, saying, Okay, okay, don't get all worked up, we'll do it some other time. You just give me a call and we'll have us a little fun. It looks like you need it to me.

He hiked the case of beer up under his arm and walked away toward the automatic doors and she watched him for a second and then another shopping cart pulled up and another behind that. She was just ringing up a chicken when the manager appeared at the side of the booth and started in about the lady who had complained. The lady said she was flirting and ignoring real customers and the manager knew it

46

probably wasn't true but you just couldn't start getting into conversations with every customer that came along because you'd never thin down the lines, and then the manager's mouth moving but Donna couldn't hear her anymore, she could only concentrate on the smear of lipstick on her wide yellow teeth and then everything spinning and for a second no sound anywhere except for a roar and far away a loud banging, like the sound of gunshots in another room, and her legs and her whole body and everything else melted away.

Roy tossed the case of beer onto the scabbed black seat in the dark interior of the pickup and slammed the door behind him and who did she think she was, he wanted to know. She should have been the one begging to come along after what he did for her. She might have thought she was something but he'd had better before and she wasn't getting any younger either, but he closed his eyes and gripped the steering wheel and there was the feel of her hair soft on the side of his face, the smell of flowers in her shampoo. He opened a beer and all down the highway that passed through town the streetlights poured into blending pools and the plastic signs for the fast-food restaurants flashed above the stunted cinder-block buildings. Styrofoam wrappers and ripped paper scurried into the gutters and then fluttered up like wounded birds as the tires spun by.

He drove past the Sonic and Dairy Queen, then by the high school and into the cloistered grid of the residential section, looking at the white houses and the windows orange with lamplight, thinking, How goddamn cozy to be there with the wife and kid around the Chutes and Ladders and the mortgage and the nine-to-five shift and the fast track straight into the grave. Oh how fucking cozy. His headlights bucked across the narrow road, banging off shrubs and tree trunks and chipped lawn jockeys and sad plaster burros and he tossed his empty beer can onto the floorboard and opened another.

Back on the highway a car full of girls shot past, five of them crammed into the brown four-door Buick, a blond one driving, plump-cheeked, her hair soft flax in the streetlight glow, and he followed them down the whitewashed drag, edging up close to attract their attention with his flickering lights. Pull over, he whispered into the windshield, pull on over goddamn it, and finally they did.

They pulled into the cratered parking lot of the Simple Simon's Pizza and he pulled in behind them and then around and up next to the driver-side window so that they were only a couple of feet apart. Her window was down already and she grinned and pushed back her hair but when she saw him the grin evaporated, a sudden sobriety left in its place. I thought you was somebody else, she said, probably only sixteen or seventeen and talking like someone stopped by the police, which rubbed Roy the wrong way and he told her a lie. I saw your taillight was out, he said, and I thought I ought to tell you before you got into trouble. He smiled. All the girls in the car bent in his direction, looking up, their faces like a cluster of sunflowers tilted in a vase. Thank you, sir, said the driver. I'll have to tell my parents about it. It's their car.

Roy looked away and then back. The blond driver had a round face and blue eyes and a small plump mouth, round and red as a piece of hard candy. Where were you all heading to anyway, he said, a party? And she told him they were just driving and if it was okay they'd just go on and do something about that taillight, and he wanted to know what their hurry was. He wanted to know if girls still liked to have fun the way they did when he was in high school and held up his beer. I got a whole case in here, he said. Why don't one of you come on aboard and help me get rid of some of it?

Oh God, the brunette in the back seat said and she punched the driver in the shoulder. Let's get out of here, and one of the others said, Is he crazy or something, and the whole carload giggled at once in their shadows. Uh, sorry sir but we gotta go, the driver said, her window already gliding upward and then the car pulling away and Roy hollered, Hey, I got enough beer for everybody! But the Buick jolted and squealed onto the road, nothing but the wide-set taillights fast disappearing and You damn fat snatch, he muttered, why don't you go on back to your pencil-dick boy-friends, and he sat back in his seat picturing the round red mouth and took a long drink of beer.

It sounded like a cough, like someone in the backyard maybe in the withered bushes hunched beneath the window and maybe they tried not to cough but couldn't help it and now they were waiting to see what would happen. Nelson crept back to his mother's room to check out the window but the backyard was only black shapes and filtered moonlight in the tree branches and he went from door to door checking the locks and all of them were locked. So it probably was nothing then, he told himself, and why would anyone be outside coughing at their house anyway? It wasn't like they even had anything worth stealing but then he remem-bered that sometimes reasons didn't matter. He went to the living room and turned up the television so that the sound filled every corner and almost drove away the sense of presences lurking outside in the dark.

All the lights in the room were on and the televi-sion family cracked their mean-spirited jokes toward each other and Nelson sat close to them but never laughed. He couldn't see why they would be that way anyway, a family supposedly, all sitting around in their two-story house with their brand-new furniture and video games and dinner at the table, and then treating each other like you wouldn't even act toward a mangy yellow cat.

Outside a car door slammed, a muffled sound above the television racket, but his mother wasn't due back for another two hours and Wesley wasn't either. The sense of someone beyond the living-room walls arose again and he turned off the TV to listen and heard a rattle at the front door and mumbled voices now for sure. He froze and the lock clicked and the door opened, the sound of wind and voices in the hall, then Maggie there at the edge of the room, only Maggie, her red hair almost electric in the bright light and his mother leaning against her like a child. She looked up, her face pale, a wide gauze bandage fixed above her eyes, and he wanted to go to her and be the brave one all of a sudden but he couldn't move at all and neither of them spoke.

It's okay, Maggie said, she just fell and hurt herself at work. I think she's been working too many hours if you ask me and the poor thing's just all worn out and aren't you supposed to be staying with somebody or have someone over here or something while everybody's gone?

Nelson looked down and I had to come on home early, he said and was glad no more questions followed because he had lied about ever having anywhere to stay in the first place. Maggie turned his mother down the hall and he got himself unstuck from the place where he stood and followed them to the bedroom. Maggie sat her on the bed without ever turning the light on and in the dark leaned over her and started to undo her blouse and he stood in the doorway until Maggie said to go on back into the front room, she'd be in to talk to him in a second. His mother would be okay, she said, it was no big deal really, she just needed some rest, and his mother finally looked at him and her voice almost too soft to hear but she said to be a good boy now and listen to Maggie and she'd see him in the morning.

In the living room he sat alone for a while and then finally turned the television on again, but he left the volume at a low murmur this time and imagined the family saying the kind things to each other they would never really say with the sound turned up.

Along the dark road that circled the lake there was nothing but emptiness and flashes of light on the water, like fallen stars broken in pieces, and Roy tossed another empty can on the floorboard and headed back toward town. The residential section set his stomach on edge and the main drag felt tainted now so he veered north and past the glass plant and the water treatment facility, and near the far edge of town a Git-N-Go sign glowed in the distance and he thought of the boy. How did the boy say it that night when he took her home? I got her. I got her now so you can just head on. That's what he said and that was all right, Roy thought. That was just fine. Because I already had her. I had all her stuff I wanted for one night.

But it was the gas sign at the Git-N-Go that reminded him because she had gone on and on about her two boys, one working the register part-time at some gas station, not a Git-N-Go but some private station, and talking about getting another job too and the other boy in grade school and what a whiz he was at geography or something like that and she went on and on and hardly shut up long enough to fuck, but she had a pretty fine body on her for someone with two kids and coming on to forty. A fine body. And he could see them now, her breasts firm in the pale spill of moonlight, the small brown nipples heaving with her quick breaths, her head thrown back and a look on her face like she was staring into some other world.

With the door pulled shut the garage was almost like a cave and you could look out at the world from its depths, a part of things and separate at the same time. Wesley liked sweeping up in there after the mechanics were gone and it was just him and the gathered racks of tires that had been brought inside for the evening, the tall red tool chests standing along the perimeter and the alternator belts dangling like sleeping bats from their hooks high on the smudged walls. There was a warmth and security, a hiddenness in the clustered shadows, unlike at the register where you were exposed and never knew when someone might burst in, a sawed-off .410 bootlegged out of view and the next thing you knew it would be all over, the oil cans leaking down from the shelves behind you, the register sprung open and you on the floor watching the light slip away.

The street outside went silent and Wesley returned to his sweeping, the crumbled black curls of oil-soaked debris tumbling in front of the broom as he pushed it slowly across the floor and then the clang out front, someone at the pumps, and he recognized the truck parked there. Instead of pumping gas the driver started toward the front door and Wesley went in and took his place behind the register. The man wore a black ball cap and faded blue sweatshirt and faded blue jeans and it was him all right. He smiled when he stepped into the light and Well, how you doing there pardner? he asked. This is a hell of a coincidence, you remember me from last night?

Wesley narrowed his eyes and nodded. I remember you.

The man put a five-dollar bill on the counter and said he needed some eighty-seven octane on pump number four but he didn't go out and put it in. Instead he took off his cap and rubbed back his hair. How's your mama doing anyway? he asked and Wesley said he guessed she was doing all right and the man looked at Wesley, his eyes squinting into black slits. The way the light was his face could have been carved out of iron. You know, I hope you didn't get the wrong idea about your mom and me, he said. Wesley said he didn't get any ideas about it at all and the man stepped up and leaned his arm on top of the register and said that was good because some people might have got the wrong idea. Because all I did was just drive her home, he said. She got into a little jam and I helped her out of it is all and then I just drove her on home.

Wesley said he appreciated it, being polite but that was all.

Yeah, the man said, it was really pretty lucky I came along when I did or who knows what would of happened, but she probably told you all about it. She hadn't told Wesley anything about it at all though and the man said he guessed he wasn't surprised about that. He said he guessed she didn't want to worry him, but if someone ever laid a hand on his mama he'd sure want to know about it. He casually removed his arm from the register and started to turn but Wesley asked him to wait a minute. What are you talking about? Who laid a hand on my mother?

The man turned back and leaned his arm on the register again. Just some old bar trash, he said. One of these fools that thinks if you buy a woman a beer she owes you some kind of favor. He looked down then back up. But I'll tell you what. I don't think that old boy is going to be doing anything like that anymore.

Wesley asked him why not and he said, Well, let's just say if you see some old boy walking around with both his eyes swole shut and his lips swole up about like a couple of tractor inner tubes then you'll know who I'm talking about.

Suddenly the man looked like a different man than the one who had first walked in. Wesley told him he sure guessed he owed him one and the man said it wasn't anything, it was just the right thing to do and just about any decent human being would have done it if they were in his shoes. By the way, he said, I'm Roy Dale, and he stuck out his hand and they shook. Wesley told his name and suggested that the gas was on him at least but Roy Dale wouldn't have it. He knew that five dollars wasn't easy to come by when you were Wesley's age. You just take good care of your mama, he said. She seems like a good lady. You tell her I asked about her too.

He started to turn away again then but again he stopped and turned back. You know, I just had an idea, he said. I bet you could use some extra money. Wesley said a little extra money never hurt and Roy Dale smoothed his mustache down at the corners of his mouth and explained that he wouldn't tell anybody else about it but Wesley seemed like someone he could trust. It won't be easy though, he said. It's farm work, manual labor and all like that. A friend of mine's got some harvesting needs done over the next couple of weekends but the money's still good.

Wesley said that sounded good but he already worked almost forty hours a week and went to school on top of that and he didn't think his mother would want him taking on any more than that right now.

Roy Dale shook his head solemnly, shadows moving across his face. You'd be making a hell of a lot more than you do around here, he said. Wesley told him he figured that was probably right but he'd promised his mother he wouldn't get another job right now.

Well, Roy said, I guess you better do what she tells you then. I guess there's no arguing there but here let me give you my number in case you change your mind. He wrote the number out on the back of a credit card slip and Wesley took it, saying he sure appreciated the offer and everything Roy had done for his mother and all like that.

That's all right, Roy said, you just give me a call if you decide you need you some extra money some time. And tell your mama if she needs anything you got the number right there. He walked out then and started to drive off without pumping the gas he'd paid for but then the truck stopped with a jolt and backed up. He pumped the gas, then waved and climbed back in the cab and drove away. When he was gone from view Wesley turned the credit card slip over in his hand, studying the telephone number as if it were some kind of code he might be able to break, before he finally folded the slip in half and stuck it into his shirt pocket, just in case.

The door was shut but she could hear them in the hall, discussing her most likely, Nelson then Wesley, back and forth and back and forth, then softer and fading away. She felt like turning on the lamp by her bedside and trying to sleep that way, the way she had as a little girl on nights of bad dreams when her father would come in to comfort her and wipe away her tears and It's all right to sleep with the light on, he'd say. Someday you have to learn to sleep with it off but when you're little it's all right. And he'd pat her arm on top of the covers but it was silly to think of it now after all these years and her father gone to cancer and her mother in another state with another man and after all she wasn't little anymore.

Now the empty half of the bed beside her stretched out like a desert she never could force herself to cross into and the black shapes surrounding, the chest of drawers, the closet door, the rocking chair and nightstand, gathered all without substance, like silhouettes cut from black paper, the gray light on the curtain neither warm nor cold, and she looked past the curtains as though for someone coming.

Take care of them, she whispered to the window,

if you're out there, take care of my boys and see that no harm comes to them. And I don't ask to get better for myself but only so I can start doing what I need to do for them again like I used to. Okay? But that's why I'm asking for help and the strength and the way to see things clear again. Because they've been trying and Nelson never complains and Wesley driving me around everywhere since I had my license revoked and trying to look after us all the time. I couldn't make it without them doing all the things they do so they don't deserve what I've been like. But I need something, I need something, because I just can't get back how I used to be. So that's just what I'm asking you for, nothing for me but for them. And the light was gray in the curtains and the cutout shapes stood silent and nothing moved beyond the glass. The voices were gone from the hall and everything empty and the only hoping left to be done was for sleep.

Wednesday Ansel rumbled up the gravel on his blue-and-chrome Harley Davidson motorcycle, dust spiraling behind, and on the front porch he and Sam slapped each other's backs in all good heartiness, and it was Sam, you old bald sonofabitch it's damn good to see you, and both of them grinning in the afternoon light, Ansel all in denim and faded plaid flannel, his gray-flecked beard hanging half down to his chest, the red bandanna wrapped tight around his long hair and the merriness lit in his eyes.

They sat on the porch with cold beer then and talked of old times, the Sunshine People and goddamn Nixon, the red-haired girls in Tucson with their little asses hanging out of those short swirly dresses and the cross-country road trip with Ned the invisible dog. And it was oh yeah and oh yeah and man do you re-member. Then finally a silent spell and just sitting and looking off toward the tree line wiping beer away from their grinning mouths, savoring the stirred feelings, until Ansel asked, So who all's coming? And Sam said it was Beeline and Jody up from Austin again and Roy Dale and his cousin Charlie.

Roy Dale huh? Ansel said then and Sam shrugged and said, Yeah well, you know, and they sat silently looking off toward the shadowed tree line, their smiles only fading a little.

While there was still good light they started on the barn. The front door stood open and the dusty light fell through cracks in the splintered boards all around the wall and rooftop. Sam unrolled the long cylinders of chicken wire across the straw-cluttered floor and Ansel would hold a length of the wire up to the two-by-fours that crossed from wall to wall some seven feet high while Sam hammered the wire into place, making a low-slung ceiling as they went, working belly to belly, their movements instinctively choreographed, nothing wasted or wanting, no awkward entanglements but a fluid repetition, even while talking, the old jokes and reminiscences all part of the machinery, and starting back up from the south wall to the north, Ansel spoke of Mexico and little Maria and the Jesus boy and the cactus painting Roy Dale stole from the blue motel and he couldn't let it go without mention of the Mexican police and their night in jail with a baggy of mescaline in his boot heel and just enough money to spring themselves come morning, and Sam said that trip should have taught him something. He said, I should have learned something right there about Roy, and for the first time that afternoon the tiredness began to creep into him and his hammer missed the nail head and the chicken wire almost fell and would have if Ansel hadn't caught it in the air.

Nelson loved the macaroni and cheese with wieners covered in sweet barbecue sauce and that was what he would have and it would be just the two of them eating dinner at the table, she thought. Wesley was gone to work and she was off early and this time she would have the whole evening with Nelson and she would be his mother just like she used to be. This was one of her good days and she even cleaned the living room and set out the football cards for the game he and Wesley had invented so she could finally learn to play. It had been a long time since she had played games with them but when they were all younger she had owned a child's spirit herself and taught them freeze tag and Annie Over and her own game she had invented called Roses Are Red. So she had done it before and didn't see any reason why she couldn't again.

When the front door opened she called to him and he told her hello but didn't come into the kitchen. He went straight to his room and shut the door and she let him stay even though she wanted him there to help set the table, plates and silverware and glasses placed just so, all in a small ritual like it used to be.

Instead she set the table herself, first his plate across from hers, then switching so that he would sit right at her elbow, not in Jack's old place, but on the other side, and maybe they would talk about school, something ordinary like mothers talked about with their boys. Or maybe going to Tulsa next Sunday to see a movie up there or even just to the riverside to throw the football or play Frisbee golf. She could even do the commentary like she used to do when they played whiffle ball in the back yard: And here's Nelson Bless up to the plate and he swings and there it goes, back, back and it's out of here, a home run, and the crowd goes wild. Only now it would just be the two of them together in Tulsa again, her and her little man. But of course he didn't like to be called her little man anymore, no, Jack had called him that, so it would be just her and her young gentleman, her escort, the two of them walking down the sidewalk under the trees by the river the way she had seen mothers do. All the words she could say running through her mind, almost like planning a speech for some formal occasion, as she set down the forks and filled the glasses with Orange Crush, his favorite kind of drink, and turned on all the lights so the drafty room wouldn't seem so cold.

When the meal was ready she called him in and it was then she noticed the slight limp in his walk. He

63

tried to hide it but couldn't quite and the wince in his eyes betrayed him that much more. She asked what was the matter and he told her nothing, he'd been playing football was all and turned his ankle a little. That was all.

Well, you come over here, she said. Sit down here and let the doctor take a look and see what the prognosis is.

He looked up at her a little uncertainly, she thought, but he sat at the table anyway, and suddenly the feeling she had been building up began to unravel as she knelt to the floor, afraid to look at how bad it might be, afraid to think about him injured in some way that needed doctoring. But that was what mothers did and mothers knew what to do when the time came, it was inside of them always, another sense as real as sight or touch and slowly she raised the pantleg and removed the worn-out shoe, so small in her hand, and eased down the sock, the movements of her hands seeming almost disconnected now, though she remembered times when they had moved with certainty and skill in anything that needed doing with her boys. The ankle, usually so thin, was swollen plump, a deep blue already inking the skin, and suddenly, like the flicking of a switch, the reality of her own boy's flesh went as vague as the wayward movement of her hands.

The sprain wasn't bad enough to call for a doctor, she told herself, settling back on her heels, but still maybe it was bad enough someone else should take a look, someone besides her. What would Jack have done if he was here? she wondered, but she knew what he would have done, he would have called her to come in because she always handled these things then. Now she only stared with no answers coming, no sixth sense to see or feel what to do, and Nelson drew his foot away and rolled up the sock himself. It didn't really hurt all that much, he told her, there wasn't anything to worry about, and all she could say was, Maybe you shouldn't play football with those boys anymore.

He only stared then, the things he wanted to say held back in his eyes, and she said, No, I mean it. People get hurt playing football. Lifelong injuries. You hear about that kind of thing all the time.

We're just having fun, he said, looking away.

Well, you let me know if any of those bigger boys are picking on you, all right? You just let me know.

Why? he said. What are you gonna do?

I'll make them stop it.

He didn't look at her or say a word but his silence told her he didn't believe there was anything she could do.

After that the dinner went slow, the cheerful conversation she had planned all dried up and blown away, and the clock ticking on the counter and him with his small head bowed over the plate as if praying for something he couldn't say out loud. But when Jack was there they always talked at the table and never had the television on. Instead they had the tradition she started of everybody saying, one at a time, what thing they were most thankful for and once Nelson said his was the moon and almost always hers was her family and Jack's was too, but now she stirred her food and had to work to keep smiling and when dinner was over she slipped into the living room and put away the foot- ball cards before he had a chance to see she had ever laid them out.

That evening at work, Wesley unfolded the crumpled credit card slip with Roy Dale's number on it and set it on the counter by the telephone. He would explain who he was again and say he'd thought it over and maybe he could take on an extra job after all right now. No reason to say anything about her or how she passed out at work. No reason to come on like he needed another job all that much at all, no, it was just that a little extra money would come in handy and what was this job all about anyway and how much did it pay? But the phone rang and no one answered and later, when it was near closing time and he'd swept the garage, he tried again but this time a woman answered, old from the weath- ered sound of her voice, and no, Roy wasn't there and she didn't know where he was and didn't have time to be taking any messages, her program was on and click she was gone. Then not more than five minutes later, just as it was time to lock the door and turn out the parking lot lights, the pickup pulled in and stopped at the pumps.

It was him, all right, Roy Dale, with a tip of his ball cap and a mechanical grin. How you doing pardner? he said when he entered and Wesley said he was all right. Your mama doing all right too? Roy Dale asked. He took a five-dollar bill out of his pocket and laid it down on the counter for gas.

Wesley said he guessed she was okay but the thing was it was a coincidence because he'd just been trying to call, he'd been thinking about that job and all and maybe they could talk some more about it after he closed up shop.

Roy Dale smiled a small cracked smile and said he thought there still might be something in the way of a job and why didn't they just discuss it over a beer. They could stop off for a beer and then maybe even go by and see Wesley's mother for a second.

I don't know about that, Wesley said. She'll probably be in bed by that time I'll bet.

Well then, Roy said, maybe tomorrow or the next day. If there's still a job to be had. I'll need to come by and take you out to meet my pardner, Sam, at his place. And maybe I'll just drop in and say hi to your mama for a second then. No harm in that, is there?

No, Wesley said, I don't guess that there is.

There was a bar on the outskirts of town Roy Dale knew and Wesley said he wasn't old enough to get into any bars but Roy waved his hand and kept driving down the main drag under the streetlights and out toward the edge of town and then down a dark road behind the refinery. Look at this dump, he said, it's a scar on the face of the land is what it is, the way they've raped this place. Shit, just a hundred years ago this wasn't anything but wild and nothing but trappers and Indians and runaway slaves. I'll bet my own forefathers were trappers roaming through these damn hills. On my mother's side. My father's side wasn't any good but on my mother's side I bet I got a great-granddaddy was a trapper living out here by himself and fuck anybody who tried to tame him down. That was how trappers were, they didn't need anybody else.

He must of at least had a wife, Wesley guessed and Roy looked at him annoyed and said, What? And Wesley explained that he had to at least have a wife if he was going to have any kids and great-grandkids and all like that, and Roy Dale nodded and said, Anyway, this pardner of mine with the land, he's a little bit odd if you want to know the truth. He's kind of like a recluse. He doesn't like questions, he doesn't like questions at all, so if you have any questions you ask me. If we go out and meet him you just keep quiet and I'll do the talking.

There was an abandoned warehouse with broken

windows along the roadside and shotgun shacks on the
other side and Wesley started to wonder if it was a mistake to come along with Roy Dale and maybe he didn't
need an extra job. His mother didn't want him to get
one anyway and even if he did he could get something
regular in town, and Roy Dale said, Here it is. Here's
the place. Don't worry about getting in. You're with me.

The bar had the name J. W.'s and a pair of tumbling red dice painted on the dingy clapboard side and
two other pickups and an old Chevrolet sat parked in
the gravel lot near a bony scrub oak. A warped plank
walk ran along the front and a small plastic Budweiser
sign flickered in the blacked-out window. Inside the
muted lights glowed dimly over the pool table and the
length of the black bar top, and a country song with
hard guitar played on the jukebox. In the far corner
three men in rumpled caps and all holding cue sticks
congregated around a square table and on the tabletop
another man crouched on all fours, a younger man
than the others with plump red baby cheeks and bangs
cut square over his small brown eyes, the mustache he
was trying to raise only barely coming in, and powerful
hands sticking out from his undersized denim jacket.
He just crouched there, his face slack at first then gathering purpose, the other men laughing and the big one
now letting out a loud bark and then another and then
a loud howl, his face tilted upward toward the lamplight, and the other men in a cloud of cigarette smoke

about to double over now from laughing. Look at the doggy, one of them said. Good doggy. Good doggy.

Holy shit, Roy Dale said. Holy fucking shit. Wesley stood back at the corner of the bar but Roy didn't waste any time and barreled into the men's midst. He knocked stumbling the man who had just spoken and at the same time grabbed the cue from his hand and the others' mouths hung open. I oughta crack your heads, Roy said. What the hell do you think you're doing? But the men just stuttered and backed away, staring warily at the cue in Roy's hand, backing away even though they were taller than he was and It was just in fun, one of them said, and the bartender said, Roy, why don't you lay that cue down, and Roy, still looking at the men who had been laughing only seconds before, just said, Do you know what this kid could do if he wanted to? He'd kick your damn ass so hard you'd have more shit for brains than you already do. And don't think he won't if I tell him to.

The men were all quiet and the big man sat on the edge of the table now, a dejected look on his face. We was just having some fun, Roy, he said. I was just doing my dog and all like that. Roy Dale shook his head and told him to come on, they didn't need this damn place and I wouldn't of thought you'd let something like this happen, he said to the bartender as he passed, I would of thought you had some concern for human dignity.

Wesley followed them outside and Roy had the other one gathered up to the side of the truck saying, What did I tell you about that kind of shit, Charlie? What did I tell you? And Charlie looking sheepish saying still that they were just having a little fun, and Roy said, They were having fun, Charlie. Goddamn it. They were having fun at your damn expense. They were making a fool out of you again. Up on that table barking like a dog. Jesus. Don't you have any self-respect? You can't let people take your pride away like that. You haven't got anything at all if they take that away from you.

Charlie bowed his head, his eyebrows cocked at a penitent angle, and Roy said, softer now, You have to learn to take care of yourself. Hell, I don't know how you made it out here when I was gone, and Charlie still looking down said, Maybe next time I'll just go right along with you. I don't care what kind of sentence it is.

Roy smiled a little now. Don't worry, I won't let it happen again, he said and he patted his friend's shoulder and buttoned the front of his denim jacket for him. Let's get out of here, he told him, and then as if he just remembered Wesley, he turned and told him to come on, they'd have to talk about that job while they drove.

Inside the truck Wesley looked at Charlie crunched in between Roy and him and he thought that maybe Roy was all right after all, and as they pulled onto the blacktop he said, When does this job start at anyway?

You don't even know how much it pays yet, Roy said. For all you know we're going to work you a ten-hour day and pay a shit wage, and Wesley paused for a second and then said he didn't figure that would happen. He figured he could trust Roy not to cheat him.

Roy laughed a stunted, dry laugh. You got a lot to learn about human nature, he said and they kept on down the blacktop and back past the sagging warehouse and beyond that the night fields where Indians and runaway slaves and trappers once lived with the earth.

In the morning Roy crawled from the rusty door of the camper shell into the grass behind the small house. He liked to tell people he lived on a ranch outside of town and that he worked as foreman for his Aunt Boots, a big operation with Arabian horses and a thirty-foot grain silo, and sometimes he could almost believe it himself when he was talking, so it was like someone had played a trick on him now with the house so old and crumbling and the camper his aunt rented to him for twenty-five dollars a month. The camper had been removed from her deceased husband's old Chevy truck and now sat in the high yellow grass, a black extension cord linking it to the house so that Roy could have a lamp and a space heater. But it was only temporary and that was all, he reminded himself, so he could stash back his money and when he got enough saved he'd never look back.

He had his shaving kit under his arm and his worn orange bathrobe on and a towel around his neck, and he went in to shower, then followed the smell of frying bacon into the kitchen. Charlie already sat hunkered at the table and Aunt Boots clattered at the stove. When she saw Roy she turned and said if he wanted any bacon he'd have to go out and get some because she'd used up all there was in the house and otherwise all he'd have to eat was toast which he could just fix up for himself.

What's new about that? Roy said. All I want is coffee anyway, and he poured his cup full and sat across from Charlie. A cold light slanted through the window and a talk show played on the radio in the corner.

So I hear you almost got Charlie in some more trouble last night out at them bars, Aunt Boots said. She turned around and gave Roy her fierce-eye look and all the deep wrinkles on her parchment face converged at once on her nose. She inhaled from the stub of her cigarette and then exhaled and the smoke rolled upward and blended with the dingy white of her hair.

Roy looked at Charlie. I almost got him in trouble? I think it was a little bit the other way around.

Charlie looked down at his plate and muttered something about how he never said anything but that Roy stood up for him, and Aunt Boots cut in with how it was low-down to blame it off on Charlie because he didn't know any better and it was up to Roy to look out for him and keep him out of old nasty places, and Roy said, Shit, it wasn't me who poured all that liquor down his mama's throat when she was carrying him. I say you should of been looking out for that, she was your daughter.

Then the fierceness flamed up in her eyes and her ravaged hands shook, and I'll say goddamn now, she said, both lips trembling, her caved chest heaving behind the blue cotton T-shirt. I will plain say goddamn you. Then her whole slumped figure lurched in clumsy anger and she flicked the cigarette straight at Roy so that it crumbled its embers down his bare chest and sputtered down the front of his bathrobe. He shot up from the table shaking it to the floor, saying, Shit almighty, you damn crazy old thing, and she was at the table now red faced and shouting, You get out of here, I don't want you drinking my coffee, I don't even want you sleeping in my camper, you can just go rot on the street you damn jailbird fool.

Fuck it, Roy said. Just fuck it. I got a hundred places I could stay and one of these times I'm really going to get the hell out of here too and where'll you and Charlie be then, huh? Where'll you be then? Who's gonna buy your damn cigarettes and snuff? Who's gonna go down to the store for your beer? And she snatched a saucer from the table and reared back, but he was already halfway around the corner when it smashed against the wall.

Through the screen door, Sam could see the motorcycle leaning on its kickstand where the morning cut back the shadows from the cool front lawn, and on the arm of the couch the familiar jeans jacket hanging and the backroom door closed and Ansel sleeping late like old times, sleeping the deep innocent sleep of a man comfortable with his conscience. He had always been one of the good ones, even there at the end of the Sunshine People when it came apart. Sam smiled over his coffee thinking of it and then beyond the Harley, far down the gravel road, Roy Dale's pickup wound into view.

Sam met him on the lawn and could see in the squint of his face he'd come for some favor. But first there was the small talk and Roy said he guessed that Ansel must be here already, nodding toward the Harley, and Sam said that he was and Roy turned his head, his silence a reproach for something he probably didn't understand himself all the way. The grass was wet with dew and Sam was barefoot and started to suggest going inside but Roy wasn't long in coming to his point about the boy and couldn't they throw a little harvesting work his way.

You know the rules on that, Sam said and Roy said that he did but maybe they could make an exception this time. It was the kid's mother, he said, he'd hit it off with her and thought maybe she might be someone he could stick with and turn his life around but the deal was she was pretty bad off financially and they could sure use the extra money, and all the while Roy's eyes taking on the deep sincerity that Sam had known for a long time and had never believed in. And I wouldn't be asking if it wasn't important to me, Roy said. You know I don't like to call in on a favor but this woman, me and her are really getting along. This might be the one.

Yeah, Sam said, I bet it just kills you to call in a favor, and he shook his head and said that maybe Roy should bring the boy out and they'd see what they could do. But I'm not taking him out to the crop, he said. Maybe I can give him something to do with the quail while we're working out there, but I don't even want him to know what we're doing.

Roy said that was fair enough and he sure appreciated it, the sincerity in his eyes fading out, and You know, he said, the other thing I was wondering was if you thought any more about that other suggestion I had. Sure would be a good way to make some more cash.

Sam took a long breath. I told you then, he said. I don't want anything to do with cooking up any crystal meth, and if you're going to be working for me, I don't want you involved in it either. That shit's no good.

I'm just saying as long as we're doing something

76

on the illegal side, we might as well get in where the real money is.

Sam shook his head. He had explained it to Roy over and over and now before he could say it again Ansel appeared on the porch, nothing but his jeans on and his beard curling down into the thicket of chest hair. Hey there, Roy, he called down sleepily. What do you know?

A distance came over Roy then and he backed away toward the truck. He didn't know much, he said, and there was a little small talk before he made an excuse to leave. I'll bring the boy by tonight, how about? he said from the window of the truck and Sam said okay. Ansel walked down from the porch and stood next to Sam, looking after the truck. That Roy sure got hard looking, didn't he?

He sure did, Sam told him and Ansel said, I'll never forget him tagging after us that first summer out here, just kind of a little guy, couldn't have been over twenty, always ready to get into something, thought he wanted to be a hippie.

Yeah, Sam said, but the only thing he really wanted to do was get high all the time and chase the women out here.

I don't know, remember when he got the big idea that we ought to make this place into some kind of ranch for runaway kids or kids with cancer or something like that?

Sam smiled faintly. That's right. I forgot about that. Of course, it never would have worked, the law would've been out here regulating the place in a second, but it was, it was a good idea to have.

Yeah, it was, Ansel said. You never know, maybe he'll have another one like that one of these days.

Behind the house stretched a narrow alley and then a fence and the empty field running to the ragged line of trees bordering the creek and then the deep red-orange sky as though some town was burning beyond, but it wasn't a town burning, it was the lights from the flying saucer glowing down there and even reflected in the bellies of the low-slung clouds directly above and Space Commander Nelson the only man between the enemy lights and the little gray house behind him. Carefully he stalked through the tall yellow grass clutching what resembled a gnarled twig but was actually a laser rifle, and his light jacket zipped to the neck, the collar turned up with the microcommunicator sewn in and Everybody stay calm, he said into the collar, I'm just going to check things out, it's probably nothing. But he knew better. He knew the lizard prince had landed. Everybody stay calm. He pinched his fingers to his lips, taking another oxygen pill so he could breathe the foreign air without a helmet or tank and crept on toward the tree line.

Then there he was, the lizard prince at the edge

of the field, nine feet tall, a brilliant red leather jacket with fringe on the sleeves and a silver bandolier crisscrossed in front, his razor teeth bared, his laser cannon gripped in his green-scaled hands. No need to panic the others, keep moving, circle around and get a better angle. But the lizard prince spotted him with his infrared vision, the laser cannon blasted and a fireball explosion sent the space commander hurtling sideways and down in the grass. What was that? What was that? called a panicked voice on the microcommunicator and the space commander said not to worry, it was all under control, it was all under control, and scrambling to his feet he charged forward, his own laser blasting, zipzipzip, and then another explosion just to the side and he dove headfirst into the grass.

Are you all right, Space Commander? cried the voice on his communicator and Yes, he said calmly. Don't worry, he'll never get past me, he'll never reach headquarters no matter what, I swear he'll never get past me, and then from beyond the fence and the alley, his mother's voice called, Nelson, time to come in. Hurry up now, I've got your dinner out on the table, and he looked back and could just see her white shirt and then her arm, and he turned again to the tree line. I haven't got much time, he said into his collar, If I don't do something now it'll be too late, and he charged again, the laser firing, and the lizard prince lurched as the blast hit his arm and Space Commander Nelson kept firing. The lizard prince jerked back and faltered, tried to reset his weapon for one last long fireball at headquarters but it was too late, another blast caught him in the chest and he dropped.

Did you hear me, Nelson? You come on in right now.

The space commander rose and surveyed the vacant field. I don't think he's going to be bothering us anymore, he said into his collar. I don't think he's going to be bothering anybody again. But the sky beyond the trees was even darker now, almost a blood red, and everybody knew that reptiles could regrow parts of their bodies and so who could doubt that the lizard prince was still out there hiding in the woods, waiting to come again and there was nothing to do but keep watching and always be ready, and always be ready to guard this small planet from evil things.

It had been coming on for several days and she had tried to fight it off but now she couldn't anymore and pulled up the rum she had laid away under the sink and set the bottle on the counter. She poured it in with Coke in a tall green glass, just like something to drink with her dinner, and when she sat down with the boys neither one said anything about it.

She smiled and handled the glass carefully, taking small sips, as she told them about her job. Nothing but small talk and thin attempts at humor. They sat in the living room, eating at trays with the television on and finally she gave up, let the laugh track drown out her words and then dabbed at her mouth with a paper towel as though wiping away anything she had been trying to say.

She never expected Roy Dale. When the knock came Wesley said he'd get it and she said, No, you and Nelson go on and finish your dinner. Still he insisted but she went ahead of him, leaving Nelson behind by himself, and then there he was, Roy Dale, on the porch in his light, almost yellow, leather jacket with the out-of-date collar and his black baseball cap and a stiff blast of cologne. She had already finished one glass of rum and Coke and now her tongue wouldn't quite connect to her thoughts right away and he spoke to her first. We meet again, he said.

Wesley stepped up beside her and said he thought they were supposed to hook up a little later on. Yeah well, Roy Dale said, I didn't have anything better to do so I thought I'd come on by early. He was still looking at Donna when he said it and for a second she felt as though she were falling forward toward his eyes and even all the way into them, and finally she asked what he was doing here, and Just a little good deed, he said. Just a little good deed.

Wesley explained about the job then and how Roy Dale had just happened to stop by the gas station one night, and Just happened to stop by, she repeated in a detached monotone. Roy Dale nodded and then told about how the job entailed taking care of some quail part-time for his partner and him in their enterprise and it was just a way to pick up a little extra money and some pretty good pay at that and he figured outdoor work would be good for the boy after being cooped up in that gas station every evening, and only some of the words came clear to her. She didn't know what it was with her mind anymore but she couldn't quite seem to concentrate. She took a pull from the green glass and said she had thought the family would stay home together tonight, she thought they'd at least have time to sit down to dinner all at once for a change, but she guessed maybe it wouldn't hurt just for a while as long as Wesley got back early enough to get his schoolwork done. Behind Roy Dale the early darkness was coming down the sky but his body formed a barrier, blocking the coolness of the evening from crossing the threshold. He touched her arm and told her, sure, it would work out fine. It was just for a while and the pay was better than they'd pay at any regular business around town because he and his partner were real entrepreneurs.

Well, she said, okay, we'll see.

Sure, Roy said and stepped inside, looking ready to make himself at home, but Wesley squeezed between them and onto the porch, sliding his arm into his jacket sleeve as he went, saying, Come on, let's go ahead and go on since you're already here, and when Roy asked him what was his hurry, he only kept walking. Roy tilted his eyebrows sadly and then followed after, looking over his shoulder. Don't worry, he told her. You can trust me. I'll fill you in on the whole operation when I come back by later.

They left then, Roy Dale and Wesley, but she could still feel the place on her arm where he'd touched her. She took a long pull on her rum and plucked the edge of the curtain and watched them cross the cracked lattice shadows toward the truck, the man giving the boy a hearty pat on the back, and he was still slender at his age, Roy Dale was, and had a certain walk about him too, the sure movement in his shoulders and hips, almost like a teenager's walk, like he was ready to take on all challengers no matter how big.

The way Roy Dale described the place, Wesley expected to find a mansion and an elaborate facility for raising quail instead of the weathered two-story farmhouse and cramped pen beside it. But the house sat well on the field, and the trees on the horizon, circling against the gathering dusk, added a sense of security that he envied. As distant as the farmhouse seemed, though, couched back in the yellow-brown grass, Sam Casey was more distant still, something secretive about him and a sadness in the eyes. He was a large man and imposing with wide, knotted hands that hinted at power even in the small gestures he made when he spoke. Roy told me you might be able to help us out around here, he said as he shook Wesley's hand and Wesley said he'd sure like to give it a try.

Roy tried to keep himself positioned between Wesley and Sam, but Sam told him to wait on the porch, he wanted to talk to the boy alone for a while. They toured the quail pen, a high-ceilinged wire cage sitting just south of the house, the quail ruffling as they passed, scurrying close to their little tin-can shelters, sometimes making a tremulous bleating, the ground around them scattered with straw and seed, and Sam Casey walked near Wesley's shoulder, his presence there warm, even gentle for someone so big. Saturday and Sunday mornings and maybe a couple of times during the week he would need someone to come throw out the feed and clean up the pen and check the water and everything would be right here, no need to come up to the house or to go near the barn. Especially the barn. It was a little old and unsafe and he didn't want anyone fooling around it. No one else would likely be around Saturday morning anyway, they had other work to do, so just stick to the quail pen and that was all and everything would be fine.

They wound back to the front of the house and it was mostly dark by now and Roy and a broad man with an enormous beard stood talking in the porch light and Who's this, another hand to help out with the harvest?

84

the bearded man asked. Sam Casey was quick to step forward then and say no, Wesley was the boy who was going to do a little work around the quail pen for him. Remember, I told you about him, he's the son of the woman Roy's seeing, and the bearded man smiled. Well, I'll tell you what, he said to Wesley, your mom must be a pretty brave woman to have anything to do with Roy.

Wesley started to ask him what they were talking about, Roy hadn't seen his mother but that once and then again tonight, but Roy nudged him with his shoulder and Never mind them, he said, they're just giving you a hard time. They don't know what the hell they're talking about half of the time.

On the far side of the closed door, he spoke what sounded like a command and that was followed by explosion sounds and gunfire and no telling what world he was living in, something far away from her, she guessed, somewhere unreachable and she wondered did he bother to think of her much at all anymore.

She ran her finger down a long crack in the wooden door frame and then left for the kitchen and another drink and then settled on the unlit concrete stoop outside the back door. There was a chill in the air and her only in her shirtsleeves but she didn't care. She could go ahead and catch pneumonia and what would it matter? Who would be the worse off? The boys could go to Ohio to stay with her mother in a proper house with someone who knew what she was doing to watch over them there. And this wasn't the heart of sorrow but a tattered self-contempt, a thicket of brambles that couldn't tear her enough. She could bleed and never be redeemed and who could she save if she couldn't save herself, and the cold wind moved in the grass along the chain-link fence and the night hard around her and lifeless and it was all her proper place.

No time seemed to have passed at all before her glass was empty again and she fixed another drink, almost all rum this time, and then wandered into the uneven field behind the house where she should have been afraid to go in the dark with no one knew what kind of man loose back there roaming along the creek side, but she wasn't afraid because you had to have something to lose to be afraid and she had nothing but a soul strangled in thorns and two boys who would be better off with somebody else, so just let the marauders come and throw her down in some gully or abyss, let them break her bones and leave her in an abandoned cistern or a caved basement where she would never be found until she was nothing but an ankle and a rib and a hank of dusty hair on a cracked-open skull.

The wind whipped her white shirt and she thought of herself as a ghost already, a spirit left to wander the grasping weeds and the twisted tree line, and the clouds above trailing wisps across the murky

face of the moon and the stars powdered on the depth-
less black. Come on out, she hollered into the trees,
come on out, I don't care, I couldn't care less, and she
sat in the brittle grass and drank her rum, ice falling
down the front of her shirt. Come on, she yelled again,
her voice trailing away, you and your homemade guns.
Come out, come out wherever you are.

And then in the distance toward the house a light
flashed briefly, a headlight on the road, someone was
coming and friend or murderer it didn't really matter.

Wesley returned to the door and said he didn't know
where she was, she wasn't anywhere in the house, and
Roy looked over his shoulder into the hallway and said,
Well, you know I was just kind of wanting to see how
she was doing, but all Wesley could figure was she must
have gone off for a walk.

Is that normal? Roy asked, and Wesley shook his
head and said that you couldn't always count on the
things she did being normal these days.

Roy adjusted his cap and Yeah well, maybe I'll
take a walk down the street and see if she's around anywhere. It's not a good idea for a woman to be walking
around on the street after dark around here, you know.

He wasn't exactly convinced that she wasn't at
home. Getting lied to wasn't anything new, but he
walked down the street just the same. There were no
streetlights for a long way down the ramshackle

neighborhood and the empty lots were nothing but ragged patches of no discernible form and he wondered what she must have been thinking the last time he saw her. He tried to read her expression but couldn't and he'd never been able to do things like that with people, tell how they thought about him the way Sam Casey seemed able to do, and how could you trust anybody when you didn't know what they were thinking? He knew what they'd done together out at the lake though, her naked breasts and soft belly and open thighs, the strange silence about her and the lost look on her face.

But there was nothing to find in the dark neighborhood and he walked back to the truck feeling thwarted and wanting to holler out loud or grab a trash can by the side of the curb and hurl it through a lighted window into the middle of some family's bedtime story, but then as he neared the side of his truck he saw a silhouette leaning against the passenger's door and a sudden lightness lifted inside him, like a foreign atmosphere he was not used to breathing.

Two different bars, warm beer and soaked tabletops, and Sure, he told her, my aunt's got her a ranch and I'm running the place for her on top of the business I got going on the side with old Sam. Big things were coming, yes, big things in the future, Arabian horses and air-conditioned stables, and he'd take her out there sometime, sometime he would when construction was done.

How about my boys? she asked him. Can they come too?

Sure they could, he told her, sure, it would be great to get some kids out there. He was good with kids. As a matter of fact he'd once wanted to work with troubled youth before he got into ranching.

Really? I used to think I'd like to do something like that too. About a million years ago it seems like now.

He leaned in close. Well, it's never too late.

You think?

Sure, he said and he touched her cheek. More beers came and again they ended up at the lake and the night just seemed to come untethered and roll away like an errant shoreline that had somehow drifted from its ships and there she floated with no recognizable landmark except the domelight above cracked open like a broken moon and the tearing inside and she closed her eyes, his breath hot on her cheek, his whiskers rasping against her, and the small tear ripped into a hole, a vast undersea canyon, that gathered everything around into its depths.

Beeline arrived before noon Friday and Jody was later getting in, his banged-up van creaking up the winding road around three and him stepping awkwardly out with that boy's smile the girls all loved. Charlie came soon after and Roy would be late he said, something to do with this new woman and all like that, and Sam said that was all right but he better be there before morning light with the rest of them or he was out and that was the rule, no questions asked, and Charlie didn't even argue. Sam knew it was better anyway because even though everybody would try to make Roy a part of them and a part of the past they shared, Roy himself could never allow it, just like he never really quite became a part of any of it before.

So they were close that night and laughed on the front porch and Charlie adapted to them fine, the way he did when Roy wasn't around, and Ansel started the stories with the one about Margaret and Beeline naked on the lopsided tractor, back before his potbelly, and they all laughed, including Charlie who probably didn't even quite understand and Jody who was only in his late twenties but had been coming to the harvest so long he knew all the stories almost as well as if he'd lived them himself.

Lanterns swung from hooks on the porch glowing with their fuzzy light and the dark hung close like the walls of a sanctuary and Sam thought of young women's brown thighs and his friends shirtless in the July sun and everybody covered with straw in the barn on the Fourth, cider and reefers and no clocks anywhere because there was no time back then, back then it was all eternity in its inner workings and how could the green fields ever grow stiff and brittle and the outer world freeze into some new ice age where eternity closed in upon itself like a black hole bound to swallow them all and not even an anthropologist left to sort through the bones.

The next morning they were all up before light and halfway across the field with packs slung over their shoulders before Roy's headlights swung around the curve and they waited while he jogged at a half-tilt across the ruts to their small circle. What's the deal, were you getting ready to go on without me? he said out of breath and You know the rules, Sam said and that was all, nobody else spoke a reproach and after a short silence Beeline clapped Roy on the back and said glad to see you and yes and yes and everybody was glad to see him, especially Charlie, and then it was into the tree line and the single flashlight beam on the narrow path and bouncing on the trunks of the blackjacks and cottonwoods and stunted firs.

At the creek bank they crouched in the morning dark waiting for first light and Beeline withdrew a leather pouch and extracted a handful of chocolate-covered coffee beans. He passed them around the circle and all partook in order to generate the energy needed for the whole day's work. It smells like rain, Ansel said and Jody said he hoped not, he'd hate to have to go all the way back to Austin and then come back again to finish off and he lit a marijuana cigarette and inhaled from it deeply, the orange glow brightening, showing on his face, and then he passed it on to Sam who passed it to Roy without taking any. They waited and Beeline draped his arms across his knees and talked of harvests from times past. Some were legendary for their abundance and some for their scarcity. The feeling of years pervaded the stories and when the cigarette came around again Sam took some, just enough for now. A cloudy grayness started across the landscape but it came slowly and it was clear that the sun would be muted today and the smell of rain thickened in the air.

Wesley came early and he breathed the feel of morning on the fields as he stepped out of the car. He collected the buckets of feed and water, everything just where Sam Casey had said it would be, and it was good to be working outside in the early morning. Even with it overcast there was a sense of newness to the earth and the sky seemed close enough to touch. The quail chattered and gamboled like play-school children and then gathered at the fresh feed with a chorus of grateful coos. The chores didn't take long and when he was done he stood outside the pen surveying the land and the farmhouse and the barn on the other side, thinking it a good place to live, but not alone like Sam Casey. It was a place for a big family, the kind of place where a grandfather lived upstairs and told stories about long ago times around the dinner table in the evening and boys could take their pellet guns into the woods on Saturday and shoot tin cans from fallen trees. He even thought about exploring the woods for himself but a car appeared up the road and he remembered what Sam Casey said about not going anywhere beyond the quail pen.

As he approached the side of his car, the little white Honda pulled up next to him and two girls looked out, the driver a brunette with round brown eyes and a lipstick smile, but it was the other one who talked. What are you doing out here? she asked bluntly. This is my father's place and he doesn't like people spying around. Wesley leaned and looked in at the freckled girl with the strawberry blond hair and the pale eyelashes around her narrowed eyes and I'm not spying on anybody, he told her. I'm working a job. I got hired to come out here and tend to the quail on Saturday and Sunday and all like that.

Well, we'll see what my father says about that, the one on the far side said and then the other one said, Aw, I'll bet he's all right. He don't look like any kind of criminal to me, and she giggled and brushed back her hair, smiling eagerly until he caught her eyes. There was a flaw down in them, a shadow that came up from inside, and all her cheerful confidence was only a thin veneer that couldn't hide it.

For a moment he felt as though he were standing inside of a secret that had its own dimensions and gravity, but then she asked him what his name was and he gathered his voice and told her. She was Jennifer Paris, she said, and her friend was Melinda. Wesley said he was glad to meet them and when Jennifer gave him her hand it felt like a handful of flowers in his.

Melinda still looked suspicious and said she was going to go up and talk to her father just the same but Wesley said he wasn't around. He was out in the woods somewhere. He was out there with Roy Dale and they had some kind of work to do before the sun even came up, and she said, Oh, looking off toward the tree line, some new worry falling across the light features of her face.

Jennifer laughed and said she bet she knew what

he was doing out there in the woods and turning sharply Melinda told her to hush. What's the matter, Jennifer said. Don't you think we can trust Wesley, I think we can, and she looked back at him, the darkness in her eyes reaching out as if to gather him in.

The dew was a long time in burning off but finally dried enough to start the harvest and they all took turns spraying each other with bug repellent to ward off the spiders and ticks. After that they stood in a circle and Sam said his thanks to the Grandfathers and the fields, the sun and the rain, everything from which they were made and to which they would return and all that nourished them in their lives in between and this was family, this was the family of our blood and bones and thank you, and then they gathered up their tarps and hand axes and scissors and in their camouflaged clothing fought through the tough jungle to their assigned sectors. Maybe it would just stay overcast, Sam told himself, and that would be better anyway because they wouldn't get so overheated and it would be harder for a DEA plane to see anything if one came patrolling their sky.

He used his heavy scissors on the plants and in the distance could hear the others, either with their scissors or axes or machetes methodically working and it wasn't long before their individual tarps began to fill and they dragged them back to the clearing and the main tarp where Charlie turned the cuttings to keep them from composting before being stuffed into duffel bags. All morning and past noon it went that way, the sound of the cutting steady and little conversation among them but sometimes Jody singing his own songs until even he began to tire and silently went on with his harvesting. It was nearly one when they started to gather again in the clearing for lunch and This is going to be a good crop, Ansel said and even though it was cool the sweat was already on his forehead and his breathing almost labored.

I don't know about that, Beeline said. He had just emerged from the tangled stand of plants, the gathered tarp dangling from one fist and a bunch of clippings in the other. We got a problem down on the southeast, he said. Hermaphrodites. Somebody didn't pull out the males down there last summer.

Oh shit, Jody said and Sam asked how many.

I don't know, four so far but there could be more, maybe ten or fifteen, could be a thousand dollars worth pretty much ruined.

Whose section was that last summer? Jody asked and he had only just asked it when Roy came out of the foliage dragging his tarp behind him and Ansel nodded toward him and Beeline said that's what he figured.

What are you all looking at me for? Roy said and Sam stepped forward because he had always been the one who had to do these things. Their eyes connected and he could see Roy knew something was wrong and then he explained about the hermaphrodites and never had to say anything about the lost money because Roy understood all that and the lost money would come out of his share but he never tried to argue or even find some excuse. He only squinted his eyes and drew everything inward and a fight would have been better than that, Sam thought, because then it would be over and they might be bruised but they could move on.

After that the harvest slowed down and once Jody tried a song but his spirit wasn't in it and it dwindled away into humming and then silence and Ansel who had always been the strongest seemed to labor more under his loads and when the ragged black clouds moved over Sam told Jody to go ahead and go back for the van and they'd meet him on the dirt road in an hour and a half and load up even if it wasn't dark yet.

That night after the duffel bags were dragged into the barn, Roy Dale left early and the mood grew lighter and Jody sang Stillwater Gypsy and Memory Ann and Never Going Back to Mexico and some of the new ones he was working on while the rain came down outside. Then Sunday they were up early clipping down their harvest and hanging the buds like green stalactites from the chicken-wire ceiling and the scent of ripe marijuana heavy in the air. They hadn't been working long when a car pulled up outside and Sam went out to find it was only the boy, Wesley, come to work in the quail pen. They talked down by the gate and Wesley mentioned meeting Melinda and Sam was sorry to have missed her.

She was a little put out with me being here at first, Wesley said, but I figured that was okay, she was just trying to look out for you, and Sam said that was probably it all right.

After that he watched the boy work for a few minutes and was satisfied that he was conscientious and trustworthy. He went back to the barn and sat down with the others. The work was going quickly but yesterday's rain would mean that Ansel and Beeline and Jody would all have to return next week to finish and that was okay, Sam liked having them there and looked forward to them coming back and as he went on clipping at the thick buds he was surprised to find himself a little disappointed that the boy hadn't asked more about Melinda. They were about the same age and if she was going to be interested in boys sometime he figured a boy like this wouldn't be bad, someone he could sit at the kitchen table with and talk to about things but even more than that, someone who would treat his daughter like a real person of her own and not the way he had seen women picked up full and thrown away empty by too many of the men he had known down through the years.

The sound of the clipping was rhythmic around

him and Jody and Beeline and Ansel joked in their half circle and Charlie sat near Ansel's shoulder, his face colored by some faint hope that he might understand their humor, and in the corner Roy Dale worked silently with his face turned to the wall.

I's that man coming over again or something? Nelson asked. She had changed into a white blouse and fresh blue jeans after work, even though it was after ten o'clock and she had a green glass full of something again. Don't call him that man, she said, his name's Roy, and anyway you should be in bed already, you've got school tomorrow. She was wearing perfume too.

Well, you've got to go to work tomorrow, he told her and she took a drink and said that was all right, she was a grown-up and she knew how to handle her time. She walked away into the kitchen and he followed her, and I don't like that Roy guy, he said as she looked into the refrigerator. There's something about him.

She closed the refrigerator door then and took a deep breath and knelt down in front of him. You haven't even given him a chance, she said. I don't want to hear you telling me you don't like somebody you don't even know, and he told her that he didn't need to know him any better and what did they need him coming around for anyway? A pained look crossed into her eyes, and she said something about how he would understand when he got older but bit her lip before she really got finished. Instead she swept back her hair from her cheek and said, Just give him a chance for me, will you? Just give him a chance. He can help us out around here and we need it. You may not think we do but we do.

A knock came at the door then and she straightened and looked down at the front of her blouse, pressed it with one hand and went to the door. He wore the black cap and the faded leather jacket and stepped in and wrapped his arm around her waist and Hey, he said, what are you drinking in there already? She shook her head and glanced toward Nelson but the man never even looked that way. He just grinned and told her he had a little something for her to try out in the truck, some real good stuff, and she frowned, pushed him away and told him to hold on while she got her coat out of the closet.

When she left the room, Roy looked down at Nelson the way someone might look at a stray dog he had only just noticed hanging around. Shouldn't you be doing homework or something? he said and Nelson said he finished his homework up three hours ago.

Well, don't get smart about it, Roy said, that kind of shit don't go over with me. He squinted his eyes and looked at Nelson more closely. You been sick or something? Your face is all pale, and Nelson said no, he hadn't been sick, that's just how he looked.

Damn, Roy said, you better get out and get you some sun then, before people start going around thinking you're a girl or something worse.

Nelson looked down at his shoes and just behind him the sound of his mother's footsteps in the hall, and I'm just going to be out for a little while, she said as she crossed the room to Roy. Now you go on and get in bed. Wesley's going to be back in a minute so you'll be all right, and Nelson said, Yes, ma'am, but he only went around the corner and stood listening, his back against the wall and shadows reaching down the floor, and he never moved until he heard the truck cough and kick over and drive away down the street.

Wesley brought up the subject cautiously, just mentioning girls in general at first. Around him the standard cafeteria business went on, the usual cliques at their little square tables, Burgess picking on a fat boy and the football team in their black letter jackets lined against the pale blue wall making wisecracks about the girls walking by. At his old high school Wesley had been a part of things but what was there to be a part of here? A small town where everyone had known each other since kindergarten and friendships were already set. So far he had only made one friend that he considered a real friend, someone he could talk to about things that mattered. James was small for his age with a bad complexion and he leaned his elbows on the table and told Wesley sometimes he thought he would never get a girlfriend at all. Maybe I'm just not cut out for it, he said. Maybe I've got something missing, and Wesley said naw, he didn't have anything missing and to just give it time. There wasn't any hurry because they had all the time in the world. There was someone out there for everyone, he said, you just have to recognize them, like allies in a war using a password and whenever they say it you know you're on each other's side.

Before this he had never thought much about that kind of thing but he had never been somewhere in the morning and seen Jennifer Paris appear all of a sudden either. He had never seen someone like that with brown hair falling down against her neck and little flushmarks on her skin at the top of her blouse and some deep wish or dream or hurt, whichever it turned out to be, half buried beneath her smile.

A burst of laughter came up from the next table over, some inside joke that had nothing to do with anything important, and he only mentioned her casually now and asked James if he knew anything about her. James said sure. He had her in his algebra class but she might as well have been from some other planet for all the chances he figured he had with her, but then he looked at Wesley and it was clear that he understood now and he looked away politely. Why? he said, are you interested in her or something?

Wesley looked off in the same direction and She seems all right, he said. I wouldn't mind getting to know her better anyway.

Well, I can tell you this, James said. She's a little on the wild side. And I heard she tried to kill herself once. I think a couple of summers ago. That was the rumor going around anyway.

Wesley nodded and thought about that as people came and went with their plastic lunch trays, their smiles as shallow as something painted on wood, and he thought maybe that was what he had seen in her eyes, the wound of that time, and maybe she had wanted him to see it, maybe she was waiting for the person who could see what it was.

That afternoon he thought that he'd missed her. The hallway was crowded with everyone ready to go home for the day, all pushing out the far door, their colored jackets and sweaters bleeding into the overcast afternoon, like nothing was different today. The floor tiles were covered with their usual dust and the lights flickered the way they were prone to do but when he turned around she was there, talking to Melinda near the senior hall lockers, just standing and talking the way a human being would do.

She wore red lipstick and a blue sweater, she had her books cradled to her chest and she turned toward him and smiled. There you are again, she said and he said, There you are too.

Her friend Melinda said something and they all talked about small things for a while, and then Jennifer asked Wesley what he planned on dressing up like, but he didn't know what she meant.

To my party, she said, What are you going to dress up like to my Halloween party this Friday night?

Melinda frowned at her then and asked her if she wasn't forgetting something, but Jennifer just glared at her before turning back to Wesley. She was dressing up as I Dream of Jeannie, she told him. Have you ever seen that old show?

Sure he had, he told her, and he'd love to go to her party too but the thing was he worked Friday nights and all like that so he guessed he couldn't go, but she reached out and touched him with one finger in the middle of his chest.

I bet you could find some way to come if you really wanted to, she said and Melinda made a face at her again, some unspoken objection that only the two of them understood, but Jennifer just smiled harder, her head tilted a little to the side, and the only thing Wesley could say was that he bet he could too.

Good, she said and patted his arm and when she walked away she never looked back until she reached the door, then she turned her head and he was still standing in the same place when she did.

Ahead Roy Dale carried a twelve-pack of beer in one hand and a huge bag of pretzels in the other. She reached out her hand and stroked him just lightly along his back as they walked and Nelson turned away. Next to him Roy's cousin Charlie looked down at him and winked. We're gonna have some kind of party tonight, he said. You oughta come.

My mother told me it was only for grown-ups, Nelson said.

Charlie nodded. I guess that's right.

But she said she'd be back from it early. She's gonna go through my candy with me.

There you go, Charlie said. That's gonna be some good eating.

They turned down the aisle where the Halloween candy and costumes were displayed and Roy set down the beer and plucked a plastic Dracula mask down, looped the rubber band back over his ears, and turned around. Here, let me at your neck, he said and she laughed as he buried the plastic face in her hair. And it was good to hear her laugh but it didn't seem to come up from as deep as Nelson had heard it before.

Look at this one, Charlie said. He was holding a

Spiderman mask in his hand. This one would look dynamite on you Nelson.

His mother walked over and said she liked it too.
You can get one of these if you want, she said. Why
don't you pick one out.

How about this one, Roy said. He was still wearing the Dracula mask but now he was holding up another, the face of a ghost. Casper the Friendly Ghost,
he said. I think this one's just made for you here
Nelson. Why don't you get it. I'll buy it for you.

That's all right, Nelson said. Wesley's gonna help
me out with a costume later on. We already talked
about it.

Besides, Charlie said, that's a kiddy mask anyway.

Just trying to help, Roy said. He put up the ghost
mask, picked up the twelve-pack and started to walk
away down the aisle, still looking like Dracula, and
even Nelson had to laugh a little along with the others
on that one.

After the grocery store they stopped off at a
liquor store and then drove into a residential section
and Nelson had to wait in the car with Charlie. What
do you think they're doing in there? he asked and
Charlie said it was nothing, Roy just had some business to take care of was all.

They talked about football for a while, Charlie
leaning with his back against the door, telling about the

107

days when he played on the high-school team even though he wasn't in the regular classes, and then suddenly he shifted and asked Nelson how come he didn't have a father.

He got killed, Nelson said. It might have seemed strange, someone else asking a question so bluntly that way but it was natural with Charlie and Nelson didn't mind talking about it. He told the whole story of how it happened and how he felt like he knew what the boys looked like who had done it and how he almost felt like he could see them waiting for him sometimes at night.

I don't understand that kind of thing, Charlie said. Tears beaded in the corners of his eyes. I'd tear those boys up if I ever ran across em, he said. All they'd have to do is give me five minutes with em.

He drew his feet up on the seat and wrapped his arms around his knees. Both of them were quiet for a moment. I basically live with my grandma now, Charlie said then, staring out the window. He said he had lived with her ever since his mother went off to Texas when he was still just a kid. She sent him a postcard once of a man riding on a giant armadillo and he didn't know where the card was anymore but he sure wished he did. He leaned his head against the glass behind him, the look in his eye like he was trying to make something out in the distance, and he guessed he had a father, he said, but no one ever talked about that.

And so Roy's your cousin, right? Nelson asked and Charlie said he was or a second cousin or something like that but they always seemed more like brothers. They'd been through thick and thin, he said.

Did he ever have any kids?

Charlie smiled at that idea. No way, not Roy, he said. Somehow I can't exactly see him being somebody's father.

No, Nelson said. I can't either.

That evening as dusk spread in the sky and between the houses and under the trees, Nelson and Ragel walked along the side of the street, their Halloween sacks swinging from their hands. My brother helped me make it, Nelson said, explaining his costume. See, I'm Space Commander Nelson. He wore a baseball cap fitted with aluminum foil, silver spray-painted gloves and hightop sneakers and carried a foil-covered dart gun in his foil-covered belt. He was Space Commander Nelson and Ragel was Sergeant Ragel of Mable Company in his green plastic helmet, combat boots, and camouflage jacket.

This helmet is just like the real soldiers wear, Ragel said.

It's dynamite, Nelson told him.

And there was nothing to be afraid of for the likes of them. No, it was the monsters who better look out tonight because let some monster come, let him have fangs and ten-inch claws, it didn't matter to Space Commander Nelson and Sergeant Ragel of Mable Company, protectors of the neighborhood. And they went door to door and only occasionally had to draw arms or dodge behind shrubs for cover as night came on, and all around lurked skeletons and witches, white-sheeted ghosts, Freddy Kruegers and Frankenstein monsters, but mostly there were vampires in black capes, slicked-back hair and whitewashed faces and eyes sunk deep in black circles, Draculas tracking the dark looking to suck the life from the unprotected, and they all had another think coming if they thought these small wood-and-brick houses and orange-lit windows were fair game for their murder. They had another think coming.

Their sacks swelled fat with candy and Nelson wasn't sure what neighborhood exactly they had strayed to when the boys on minibikes descended. They were older boys, junior-high boys, one with a black helmet and the other bareheaded, fat with a crew cut, and at first they sped down the sidewalk on the other side of the street kicking a skeleton's sack and causing witches to scatter toward the closest lit porch, their black dresses flying around their legs. Nelson and Ragel barely had time to draw their guns when the minibikes turned on them but plastic weaponry was useless now and nothing to do but run and the sack banging against Nelson's leg and the cold air stinging in his lungs as the shrill

engines buzzed behind and then a kick to the side
knocked him sprawling. Ahead Ragel stopped and
wheeled around and the minibikes were wheeling back
too as the boys struggled together. Come on, come
on, let's get over that fence, Ragel yelled, they can't
follow us over a fence, and without looking around
both scrambled for the chain-link fence, Ragel
pulling Nelson over, the engines whining behind and
Halloween sacks hung up on the railing. But Ragel was
right, the minibikes were stranded back on the lawn,
and the two boys sat shoulders together behind a hedge,
their chests heaving and their weapons nowhere to
be found.

How did I know you were gonna bring your boy along?
Roy asked.

All I'm saying, she said, is I don't want my boys
around if you're selling that stuff. I don't care if you
do, I think it should be legal anyway, but I just don't
want my boys around it.

Okay, he said, all right.

And the other thing, she said, I've got to get back
in time to help Nelson sort through his candy.

You know what you oughta do? he asked. Fix up
your hair instead of letting it hang down limp like that
all the time. Put some curl in it or something.

I told him not to eat any of it before I checked
it all out, she went on, because what if there's razor

blades or needles in there? People do that, you know, and Roy looked away from the windshield, pulled the marijuana cigarette back from his mouth, and Don't worry about that shit, he said, this town isn't big enough for maniacs like that. He passed the cigarette to her and she sat looking at the end burning orange between her fingers. There's maniacs everywhere, she said and then raised her hand, inhaled deeply, and chased the smoke with a drink of rum.

You ever thought about going blond? Roy said but she didn't answer. The marijuana paranoia began crawling up inside and all down the street, the garish lights of the fast-food places grinned just the way she thought the maniacs would and she could only guess what kind of sick ideas took up their hiding places in the speed and confinement of the anonymous cars flying past. She inhaled from the marijuana again anyway, hoping to break through to somewhere else, and still the people around remained separate, unintelligible beings, blanks and ciphers and she herself nothing but a jagged fragment of fear surrounded by lies and excuses, and who was this even sitting beside her now? What did she really know about him? But the rum went down warm and there was plenty more, all of it needed to get to that pinpoint circle in the front of her brain away from the chasing panic, and Roy said, There's a club up ahead that stays open after hours if they know you good.

Do they have rum? she asked and he said sure, they had anything you wanted.

Finally Eddy arrived to finish up the evening shift. Wesley had never taken off early before, but he had a little extra money now and Eddy owed him one anyway. And besides this was something special for a change. I feel like I recognize her from somewhere else, he told James as they drove to the Halloween party. I feel like I met her in another lifetime.

You probably did, James said. I believe in those things. I believe we go from lifetime to lifetime until we find what we're supposed to find. It's like a mystery story, only you're looking for your real life instead of a murderer. And Wesley was silent then and stayed silent until they came to her street.

The house was large, two stories and clean white, and he hadn't expected anything so grand. The party was mainly in the wide, sloping back yard, all around girls in short-skirted witch outfits and sexy space alien costumes and boys dressed as cowboys and hobos and rock stars and toward the bottom of the yard evergreens crowded against shadows and several stragglers gathered there, among them Melinda dressed as a hippie, but no Jennifer Paris. On the way back it was hello and hello and not bad how are you and Melinda smiled, her eyes soft blue and inviting in a shy kind of way, and everything about her now friendlier than when they had met at her father's place.

I wondered whether you would come, she said.

I wouldn't miss it, he said and introduced her to James and she said yes, she already knew him. Around them the partiers milled and Burgess in a red cape and horns wired to his head hollered, Whiskey, who wants whiskey, and one of the girls told him to shut up his mouth.

Wesley stood on the verge of the shadows by Melinda and they talked a little, his smile uncontrollable and so wide it made his face tired. So what do you think about my father? she asked and he told her she was lucky to have someone like him with his farmhouse and land and the quiet way he held his confidence, everyone should have someone like that, and she looked up at him, straight into his eyes, and something passed between them, though he couldn't say what it was, not anything like romance but something with weight and substance just the same, an understanding that ran beneath words like an underground stream, and they were silent for a moment before he looked back across the lawn and asked where Jennifer was.

Uh, she said, well. She shifted from foot to foot and hugged her arm to her side. I guess she's around here somewhere, she said. I guess she went to get some punch or something, and Wesley said he might as well go get some himself before Burgess got to it with the whiskey and Melinda put her hand on his arm. You know she's with someone, don't you, she said. He looked at her, uncomprehending, and a kind of sadness laced her eyes and she said, She's got a date. I guess she really should've kind of made that clear but that's just Jennifer. That's just the way she is.

Oh, Wesley said and all around the party was frozen for a second and when it moved again everything had gone hollow. Yeah, he said. Well, I kind of thought she might be with a date but I just wanted to say hi and all like that, that's all. I can't stay long anyway, I have to make sure my little brother got home all right.

He wandered away from her then and James hurried just behind asking where they were going and Wesley just said, Anywhere but here.

On the front lawn someone stood in a sheet with eye holes cut and someone else walked behind with a jack-o'-lantern head and children paced the sidewalks in little plastic costumes. The trees were almost bare and the tops of them bled off indistinguishable from the night and That's just the way she is, Wesley thought, that's just the way she is, and then behind him he heard his name called and he only wanted to hurry away but something made him turn, and there she was in the I Dream of Jeannie outfit, the billowy pants and bare midriff and a little red fez marked by a crescent shadow where the Shriner emblem had been removed, and You aren't running off already, are you? she asked.

She smiled and he said he was thinking about it, he had somewhere to go, and You want any company? she asked and the substance of the world came rushing back in.

It was late by the time they parted and Nelson said, Don't worry, I've walked home this way a million times before. He refused to even stop by the house because he knew Ragel's parents would insist on driving him home and then what if they saw his house the way it was and maybe even his mother with her green glass waving and the man there in his leather jacket? What if they saw all that, would they say, Ragel, don't go around that boy and his family anymore, they're not the kind of people you need to know.

Besides he knew a way home where there were people's houses and some stores and streetlights most of the way, and the worst was over with the boys on the minibikes, the worst was over, and the breeze made a rattle in the leaves that still clung to the trees and rattled even louder in the leaves in the yards and gutters and the streetlights were silver on the asphalt, like a stream flowing out of the dark. His candy bag banged against his leg and Space Commander Nelson calling Mission Control, he said into his collar. Mission Control? Can you read me? But there was nothing but the rattle of the leaves and then somewhere behind it, the tinny whine of the minibike.

116

He walked faster and a store sat right around the next corner, a store and people and cars, but the minibike buzzed closer and then there he was, the boy with the crew cut, circling slow and then stopping, straddling the bike, the engine humming. You're the kid with that nigger while ago, aren't you? he said, his small eyes narrowed and Nelson tried to walk around but the boy said, Where do you think you're going? You're not going anywhere. He toed down the kickstand, stepped off and walked up to Nelson and said, I asked you a question. You're the kid with that nigger while ago, aren't you, and Nelson looked down and then up at the boy's eyes sunk in their fat cheeks. I don't say that word, he said. That's a stupid word and I don't say it.

What word's that? the boy said. What word don't you say?

You know, Nelson said and started away but the boy caught his arm and Nigger? the boy said. Is nigger the word?

I'm just going home, Nelson said. Just let me go.

The boy held onto his arm and bellied close to him. I'll let you go if you tell me your friend's a nigger, he said. You just say that and you can go on anywhere you want to go. Say, My friend's a nigger. Just like that.

Nelson stood still, looking past the boy's shoulder. There was a streetlight at the end of the block. Are you going to say it? the boy asked and Nelson shook his head.

The hell, the boy said and wrenched Nelson's arm, swinging him to the side, then around and onto the grass and then he was on Nelson's back pushing his face into the ground and You're going to eat this grass till you say it, and Nelson said No, I'm not, I'm not ever going to say it. He's my friend and I'm not ever going to say anything against him and you can't make me, and the boy ground his face harder into the dirt and grass and Say it, say it say it, he ordered but Nelson clenched his lips shut as tight as he could. The boy hauled him around and the square fist pumped once straight into his eye, and You going to say it now? but Nelson shook his head and the tears burned and his lips trembled even though he didn't want to show it and the boy hit him again and Nelson clenched his eyes shut and then opened them and stared into the boy's small eyes and I'm never going to say it, I'm never going to say it and you can't make me, he cried, his voice trembling beyond his control now, and the boy looked bewildered for a second, then Look at the baby crying, he said, the baby's crying, but there was no force in his words now and Nelson cried, I don't care, I don't care I'm not ever going to say it, and his voice trailed off into sobs.

The boy stood up then and still straddling Nelson said, Shit, I don't have time to waste on a little crying baby, and looking lost for a second, wavered above as though waiting for someone to tell him what to do next. Nelson shut his eyes again and in a moment the minibike revved and then its whining dwindled down the street and the boy shouted something along with it but it didn't matter what it was.

His candy bag lost, he walked the rest of the way with his hands in his pockets and at home the driveway was barren and the lights all off inside. But that didn't mean she wouldn't be home, it didn't have to mean that at all, she could be inside asleep already or listening to the radio in the living room the way she sometimes did but he could feel the emptiness as soon as he stepped through the door. Still he went to her room and stood looking at the emptiness there, the unmade bed, the gray light in the curtains and across the cluttered dresser, the clothes tangled on the floor.

But Wesley would be back soon, he could count on that at least and he sat on the floor, his back against the wall. He could count on Wesley all right and he touched his fingers lightly to the swollen flesh under his eye. A tree limb banged against the window somewhere and soon there would be the sound of a car on the gravel and if you couldn't count on that then you couldn't count on anything anymore.

Wasn't there something you were going to do? she asked and Wesley said yes, but he couldn't remember what it was. She laughed and threw open the door and ran down the gentle hill of the technical college campus, her I Dream of Jeannie pants billowing and her ponytail bouncing between her shoulder blades and there had never been anything prettier in the history of the universe, that and the way she laughed.

All the geese scattered and a swan fled into the water, its big wings spreading then folding as it sailed away into the dark center of the pond. At the edge of the water, she turned and If I was going to be anything it'd be a swan, she said. They're the most beautiful things, don't you think? And he said he thought she'd make a good one. She sat on a long flat rock, stretched out her legs, and looked down at them admiringly. It's kind of cold, she said, but I don't care. He sat beside her and he didn't care either.

A rusty smell came up from the water and hung as close as the darkness and he didn't know what she said then but the side of her face next to him shone like a new planet with its own kind of gravity pulling him in. The swan circled by and the geese settled back and a cow lowed in one of the rolling pastures beyond the desolate Highway 51 loop. She leaned her head on his shoulder, but all he could think to say was, Melinda said you were with a date tonight.

She pulled away and he immediately wished he had said anything else but that. She did? she said. Well, I guess I'm not surprised.

He asked how come and she told him she wasn't

surprised because Melinda had a little crush on him if he wanted to know the truth and he shook his head and said, But you all are friends, and Jennifer said it didn't matter when it came to boys you couldn't trust Melinda.

But you're friends, he repeated. You don't sabotage your friends, no matter what, and she just said, Well, some people do, and he looked at the pond, still shaking his head, trying to make the Melinda he'd just talked to fit such an idea.

But let's not talk about that, Jennifer said and leaned back against him and now his arm went around her shoulder almost automatically, as if she needed comfort for having been betrayed by somebody close. They sat that way for a long time and the air at the pond was cooler and she huddled closer. He ran his fingers lightly along her forearm, her skin soft, and near the wrist, just at the lines under her palm, a scar traveling up from her hand and across the blue veins, a narrow white ridge that didn't make sense in the middle of her warmth and breathing. He touched the scar and moved his fingertips down its length but he didn't know what to say. She turned her arm over and leaned into him and he kissed her and then her hand came up to his chest, a soft pressure that seemed to measure the swell just behind his breast bone, her lips full and soft and her hair smelling like apple candy.

The kiss lasted and when it was over she lay her

head against him. He thought she might say something about the scar but she didn't. Instead she told him that she knew they hadn't known each other that long but she could tell things and he was different.

Different from what? he asked.

The rest of the high-school boys I know. You don't seem like you're caught up in all those little games like they are.

I guess I'm not.

Me either, she said and he said he was glad about that.

So you work for Melinda's dad? she asked him and he said that he did.

Is it true he grows marijuana out there?

What?

Melinda said how she thinks he might be growing pot out there and I was wondering if maybe you might of got some.

I don't know anything about that, he said. If he's growing marijuana, then he's keeping it to himself.

But wouldn't you like to get some, she said. Some killer stuff and a bottle of tequila or Strawberry Hill. I mean, don't you ever feel like just getting out of your head?

Not really, he said. I don't want to be messed up if something happens, if something goes wrong and I've got to be there.

I don't know, she said, disappointed. If something

went wrong then I think I'd want to have something, like at least some beer or strawberry wine. She drew her head away and the warmth went with her and You know what? I better be getting on back. I mean, it's my party and all. People are going to start wondering where I went off to. She stood and the breeze fluttered in the billows of her pants. We'll have to come back down here some time, she said, and he said that he hoped that they would. Her smile widened and she pushed back her hair and just for a second he caught another glimpse of the scar on her wrist.

B reaking the harvest up into two weekends was riskier but that didn't matter so much to Sam Casey. What mattered was he had his friends back and the rooms full of talk again on Friday night and Ansel at one point standing on the coffee table reciting a passage from Winnie the Pooh that he knew by heart. The next morning they were crouched in the dark again, the sound of the stream soft beside them and Beeline passing around the chocolate-covered coffee beans, only this time when the sun rose no clouds appeared to obscure it, and Thank you Grandfather for the sun in our bones and all on the deep earth and in these plants, Thank you, Thank you.

They went into the field then and soon the chuff-chuff sound of the scissors and hatchets began and only Roy Dale failed to be exuberant in the work. The hermaphrodites had been his own fault and if anyone else had made the same mistake then money would have been deducted from their cut too, but Roy never took setbacks lightly and dragged through the field with ponderous steps and tight jaws, while the others moved in the sunlight and wind almost as though they were part of the plants themselves and Jody sang every Gypsy song he knew.

Near noon a plane passed over and they all crouched low in the foliage as the motor sputtered closer but it was only a biplane, someone's weekend hobby, and Never mind it's only the goddamn Red Baron, Beeline said and everyone laughed from relief as much as from the joke.

When they broke for lunch, Ansel was the last to emerge from the field and Sam noticed a tiredness in his shoulders, a slouch that had never taken shape there before, and maybe it was from trying to take up the slack that Roy Dale made or from the factory job he worked during the week to keep up his family or maybe it was even from being almost fifty years old. But no not that, Sam decided, surely not that, and sitting down beside him Ansel just shook his head and grinned. Whoo dogs, he said and that was all. And he was okay, Sam told himself. They were all okay.

After lunch Ansel only worked harder, cutting into more of Roy Dale's sector and hauling up the filled tarps to the dumping station where Charlie worked, and sometimes Sam would meet him there and How you doing? he'd ask and Ansel would say, Coming along, coming along, and once he worked his left arm in a cocked windmill motion and rubbed at his neck. A little sore, he said, but coming along.

By four everyone was done but Roy Dale and Ansel. The rest stood waiting in the clearing talking lightheartedly about the work, Jody hardly fazed but Beeline breathing hard and sweating, and then Ansel appeared at the edge of the clearing, an enormous filled tarp slung at his shoulder and Sam smiled and called out, Everybody just about finished back there? But Ansel stopped, a strange half-smile carved lightly on his face, his eyes filled with something like pity and then his legs buckling so that at first he looked as though he was walking down some crumbling stairs but there were no stairs and his knees crashed into the ground and he dropped forward, face down on the tough stubble and lay there still, the full tarp burst open beside him and behind him the tangle of plants and the flat blue sky and everything still as the earth's first day, except for the slow, dull chop of Roy's machete somewhere in the distance.

Donna wouldn't go to the bars with Roy Dale that night. She said she had let her boy down. She said, You should see his eye, he looks like he's been in a prizefight, I'm not going anywhere and leaving him here by himself. I'm through with that, and he said, But you don't understand. Somebody died today.

She was tight lipped and determined though,

and standing at the door he felt he could almost hit her. He could push that staunch expression down her throat and don't think he wouldn't. Someone had died and she wouldn't even listen. She'd let him go out to the bars and drink by himself, so don't think he wouldn't hit her if he wanted to. But instead he just said, Fuck it, and shoved his clenched fists into his pockets and walked down the porch steps without another word.

And I don't want you letting Wesley work around those pot growers either, she called after him, and Whatever, he said to himself, whatever, and let her stay in her bed by herself, let her dry up and blow away, let her come begging to him next time she needed something to hold onto.

At J. W.'s the jukebox played too slow and the singing came out like the moans of condemned souls lost in the wrong dimension. The pool players paced in their circle of smoky light, and removed from them Roy leaned over the bar with a pitcher before him and beer foam on the sleeve of his jacket. Catercorner sat a woman with gray teeth crossed slightly in front and her saddlebag purse on the bar. Between sips on a longneck bottle she sang along with the jukebox ghosts, Just call me Angel of the Morning, a circle of smoke hovering around her matted brown hair.

You look like that woman from the movies, Roy told her, and she stopped singing and looked at him, her eyes small and dull. What woman? she asked and he said, You know, that sexy one.

She looked confused then, her face all screwed up, but Roy got past it with a question about her saddle-bag purse and she was no conversationalist but that didn't matter, he did the talking and it wasn't long before he was off on Ansel and no one had asked Ansel to take on any extra work anyway. It was his own idea and he'd always been like that, the kind who tried to make you feel guilty by doing more than his share or talking about how the world ought to be, and that time in Mexico, it was just a crazy spur of the moment idea to take that painting off the motel room wall and who would have thought the Mexican cops would show up and throw them in that piss-stained little jail and as for Margaret that was between Roy and Beeline and what business did Ansel have coming in with his opinion about how to treat people? Him and Sam, they were a pair, they might as well have been a couple of holy rollers with that self-righteous line of bullshit they put out but they didn't do the jailtime for possession with intent that other time either. Hell no. Sam and Ansel and everyone else were out walking the fields, singing songs on the front porch with Jody and taking vacations to the Grand Canyon or somewhere, Ansel and his whole family like a bunch of Baptists from the suburbs or something. By God.

The woman only smoked and drank and stared

dully through the smoke and finally Roy stopped and said, Shit, why am I telling this nonsense to you? I mean, all I really want to know anyway is do you want to fuck?

The music had stopped by then and the words almost froze in the air and at first her face was blank but then almost mechanically she turned to the pool tables and hollered, Daryl, Daryl, you know what this damn guy said to me?

Daryl was almost a head taller than Roy and he didn't like any of this business about do you want to fuck being said to his sister, he didn't like it one bit, and I see you don't have that big-ass friend of yours here to protect you this time, he said. He leaned down close to Roy, his face red and meaty with a little curlicue of black hair pasted on the forehead and his small gray eyes sparked with a familiar fierce glee. Roy had dealt with it before and he said, How about this, how about I pull your face out through your asshole. If I can tell which is which.

Daryl's hands were at his collar then and Roy swung his beer glass into the meaty jaw and Daryl staggered but still clutched tight to the collar, hauling Roy off the stool. Then someone else was there or maybe three more or four, it didn't matter, Roy swung his fists whichever way he could and connected and missed and connected again, tearing his knuckles on something ragged and hard, but too many arms were at him now and he smashed headfirst against the pool table edge and then to the floor and the next thing he knew he was flung outside on the gravel, the dust in his mouth and rocks cutting his face, and someone had his hair and flailed his head into the ground again and again and a kick in the ribs and another and another and something hot in his eyes, he guessed it must be blood because everything went red and the kicking went on but it was almost like something happening far off to somebody he barely even knew.

When Donna lay down that night and closed her eyes, the haunted people descended, grotesques with tumors humped over their eyes, deforming their noses, crusted lips over broken teeth and bleeding gums, scaled wings and tumescent hands outstretched, hovering over her, soundless but grasping, and she sat up in bed and stared at the window, focusing on what was real, what could be touched, the curtains and the hard, cluttered top of the dresser, the knob on the closet door, anything to drive back the phantasms and this was it, the border-world of the delirium tremens, and it was late before she finally slept and had only just drifted off when the pounding sounded outside.

She knew it was him and she knew he wouldn't leave without seeing her so she went to the door and opened it slowly. There he was with the blood caked in the corner of his swollen eye and down his face and spattered on the leather jacket, his lips bruised and misshapen as grotesquely as any hallucination, and she was back in that other doorway with the blood in front of her and the last faint breaths on her husband's lips when the world turned inside out and left a part of her trapped on the wrong side of it, in that other doorway on that other night.

I had some trouble, Roy Dale said, stumbling into her and she saw him again in front of her and felt his hand on her arm, grasping weakly and then his face on her shoulder. I think I got a busted rib, he said.

What happened? she asked him but he only coughed and said that he better sit down.

Wesley was in the kitchen doorway then and asking questions but she told him to go on back to his room and in the hallway Nelson, a small shadow against the wall, said, Mama, did somebody shoot him?

No, she said, No one's been shot. He was just in a fight, I think. Now you and Wesley go on back to bed.

In the bathroom she dampened a washcloth but when she brought it to his face the blood was all she could see and the floor moved beneath her and the walls started to fall down and she had to step back and steady herself against the sink. She couldn't look at him then and handed him the washcloth. Take it, she said. Get yourself cleaned up. I can't do it, I've got to go lay down. There's alcohol in the cabinet and Band-Aids.

He tried to call her back but she was already out the door and down the hall. She sat on the edge of the bed and there was blood on the shoulder of her T-shirt, specks of it smeared down the sleeve, and she tore off the shirt and threw it against the closed closet door. The only light came from outside the window and she hugged the pillow and drew the covers up around her shoulders and when the door opened she shuddered at the sound.

He never spoke and the light didn't fall across his face so that he could have been almost anybody as he lay down beside her. He was nothing like he had ever been before but lay quiet and for a long time they were quiet and then she asked him if he wanted to tell her about it, but he said he didn't think so, he just wanted to be with her right now, and moved his head down and rested it against her breast. She folded herself to him then and he was submissive in her arms, no kisses or rough fondling, just stillness, and she stroked his hair and closed her eyes and listened to his breathing in the dark.

Do you think somebody tried to kill him? Nelson asked.

Wesley sat on the edge of the bed, his silhouette black against the window, and No, he said, I think they just wanted to mess him up pretty bad.

The way that boy did me?

Kind of like that.

They were quiet for a moment, then Nelson asked, Why do people do like that? And Wesley said he didn't know, some people were just mean, he said. They didn't care anything about anybody, and then they were quiet again for a while before Wesley said, I should of been there. I should of come over and driven you home.

That's all right, Nelson said. It wasn't your fault.

Well, no one's going to get away with doing like that to my brother, Wesley said. I don't care where we live, we don't have to put up with that kind of sorry stuff.

Nelson looked down and then back up. You don't have to do anything, he said. I mean, to that boy. If we found out who he was and all, you don't have to get him back or anything. It'd just probably get you in trouble then.

Wesley didn't move or speak. In the darkness, Nelson could discern no expression on his face. After a while he turned sideways and cocked his leg up on the bed and lay his arm across his knee and Nelson knew that he was thinking about things. In the kitchen the refrigerator motor cut on and then a car went by outside and it wasn't so quiet anymore and Nelson said, Do you think we'll ever find those guys?

What guys? Wesley said, turning his head.

You know, Nelson said. Those teenagers with the homemade gun.

Wesley leaned back on his bed then and I don't know, he said. I don't know if we ever will or not. I used to think I was going to track those guys down but that was when I was a kid.

Nelson lay his head back on the pillow then and that was something he never knew. He never knew how you could grow up to understand the world less than you did before.

L orna Feather shook back her serape and held up her tanned hands to the sky, her long blond hair falling back as she tilted her head, wrinkles creasing down her sunburned cheeks. She said, Here he is and here and here. The wind walks and he walks, the grass reaches to the sun and he reaches to the sun.

Only the grass was dead and reached nowhere, the bland sky was as gray as limbo must be and the wind too cold for bare arms like that and Ansel should be standing here and laughing and not in a can waiting to be hurled into the lake. That's the way it should be, Sam thought, Ansel should be standing here and laughing.

But Lorna Feather said, The dimensions of the world are deep and many layered and come, come, we will be one. The earth is in us and we are in the earth and come, come. We are the water and the fire. We are the spirit and the flesh. We are and we are. Come, come, we will be one.

The gusts pulled at her colored serape and her blond hair whipped away from her face. All around people stood silent and too mournful for Ansel and anyway Sam had known her when she was only Lorna Corkle the perpetual graduate student and maybe he had said such prayers himself and maybe other times the earth and he were one but what did prayers mean now with no heart left in the world to be part of?

Ansel had been a boy once with long chestnut hair hooked behind his ears and more joy than his eyes could contain, powerful arms and large hands, broad chested, and always a wisdom about him, even in his youth, a depth, an ancient spirit and merriness. He could juggle oranges and carve horses from driftwood, he could drive the breadth of Texas without tiring, he could roof a house and overhaul an engine, he could make you laugh with a cock of his eyebrow and he could look you in the eye and say he was sorry.

Terry, his widow, leaned into Sam's side and he wrapped his arm around her shoulder. The lake was gray with rolls of white wavelets. Trampled yellow grass rimmed the edge and a narrow gray pier extended over the water and on the far side twisted trees struck against the sky and Lorna Feather paced before the crowd, over one hundred people all gathered from the parking lot down to the marina and over to the jetty on the south. Her eyes were as gray as the lake and the sky and she spoke in rhythms bordering on song but Sam barely heard her now as he watched the faces all along the front row where he stood, Ansel's coworkers from the lock factory, middle-aged women in denim and patchouli, remnants of the Sunshine People side by side with stock brokers or bankers or whoever they were, Ansel's two boys with Terry and the older boy from his time with Joanne now almost grown, faces and faces, all the somber expressions, a parade of years and sorrow, whole lifetimes poured into this one moment on the water's edge, and what if someone just broke away from the crowd and pushed past Lorna Feather and sprang down the narrow pier, peeling away clothes, kicking off shoes, and then a high arch, a jackknife maybe, or even a cannonball, and down, splashing into the gray lake, and everybody all at once following until the water churned and flew with flailing arms and legs and who cared how cold it was. But no one moved, no one moved except to shift their feet or raise their hands to cough, and Lorna Feather went on, because the only one who could ever have led such a revolt was gone away.

Jody sang Stillwater Gypsy and that's when the tears broke loose and then from the end of the pier Terry scattered the ashes down onto the waves and that was the end. Sam rode back to Wichita Falls with Terry and at her house the gathering was more intimate, and she and Ansel's two boys stood talking by the stockade fence in the back yard. There was an oak tree and a tire swing and a grill and everything almost Ozzie and Harriet here in the ranch-style brick neighborhood, a different world than he had ever envisioned for Ansel and Terry. It had been so long since Sam had come down for a visit and it was strange now to be standing among the gold upholstery in this family's home so much the same as the one he had grown up in years ago in Kansas, back in his crew-cut and coonskinned boyhood. He had been wild to get away from those houses then, nothing would do but to leave them behind, and now he couldn't quite remember why.

In the shadowed hallway, away from all the people with their paper plates of fried chicken balanced on their knees, photographs hung in no discernible pattern or order, some tacked or taped and others framed against the simulated wood paneling: Ansel and Sam standing in front of the old geodesic dome when it was new, Beeline with a black beard and an almost athletic build, Gordon the Labrador retriever, Sam in a straw cowboy hat and Ansel shirtless holding up a catfish, standing in the sun, motorcycles, pickup trucks and microbuses and a sky blue Rambler with red-striped wallpaper on the hood, the Sunshine Girls giggling and toppling over one another, their long hair parted in the middle, tans and peasant blouses and cutoff jeans and then all the Sunshine People together, the last group picture, and who could have held the camera because it looked like everybody was there, even Roy Dale standing off to the side, his face turned down.

There were later pictures too, but Sam lingered over the Sunshine days because they were the strongest inside him and some of the people in the newer photographs he didn't even recognize. Terry came up behind him and put her arm around his waist and they went outside and sat on the edge of the wooden deck. You all have a nice home here, Sam said. Real cozy.

I don't know, Terry said. It looks different to me now. All hollow. I guess I'll have to get used to looking at it all over again. She pulled her hair away from her face and she looked scared, her eyes did.

It was hard to look at her and Sam stared toward the fence and if he could have traded places with Ansel, if he could have been the one floating away on the gray waves so that Ansel could be back among his family, he would have done it without another thought.

Anything you need, you just let me know, he said. You know Ansel has a good-sized share of profits coming in, bigger than usual. It was a great crop this year, we didn't lose a plant, and as soon as I can I'll send you what you have coming. And anything else, you just let me know.

Her head was on his shoulder then and I feel like I'm falling, she said. I keep reaching out to grab ahold

139

of something but there isn't anything there, nothing but air, and nothing to even break the fall.

Sam wrapped his arm around her. You've got the kids, he said. That's one thing, you've got the kids, and she didn't say anything but they sat quiet and then without another word she went inside and later Sam saw her through the patio window kneeling with her hands on her boys' shoulders and she was smiling.

Wesley hung the tin bucket on the nail outside the quail pen and shut the gate behind him. The sun sat just above the treetops and the immaculate afternoon light cleansed the landscape and all the structures of the farm. Down on the winding road the dust rolled away from the back of a car, her car, gliding and low-slung, the sight of it promising and ominous too, like a wind moving in ahead of a storm.

He had just been thinking about her and what James had said about Weber. James had stayed at the party when Wesley and Jennifer left, and he'd run across Weber reeling drunkenly across the lawn, spitting out curses. He'd looked up all of a sudden and his date was gone, he said morosely. She'd just taken off without saying a word. And it was Jennifer, that was who his date was supposed to have been, and he'd be damned if he'd ever spend a cent on her again.

Her car pulled up beside Wesley and she smiled like nothing was wrong at all. Melinda sat next to her and waved but an uneasy look hung in her eyes. He told Jennifer he'd tried to call and even left a message with her mother, but she never stopped smiling and only said that her mother must have forgot.

He said that he figured it was something like that. He figured it had to be something after the way Halloween night had been, except for one thing, and he told her about Weber.

Oh him, she said, looking away out the windshield. He's been chasing me all over ever since we were sophomores, and that was the only explanation she gave and Melinda just stared down at her shoes. Wesley stood looking for a moment but he might as well have been staring at the stone faces on Easter Island, and just when the moment was growing too long, she pushed open her door and stepped outside. She was only a few inches away. I was hoping you'd be here, she said, looking up into his eyes. I told Melinda I thought you'd be working at her dad's place this afternoon, and Wesley could think of nothing else to say but that he was glad she had come.

So it's just you here, huh? she asked. Her eyes flashed but he still couldn't read them and told her that he had come out to lend a hand while Sam Casey was at a funeral in Wichita Falls and as far as he knew no one else was around. Roy Dale had said something about showing up but his truck wasn't here.

She asked if he ever thought about going up to

the barn to see what was there, and he told her he wasn't supposed to go anywhere but to the quail pen. That's all right, she said, stepping by him, but since no one's around maybe we should go exploring, I mean just for a while.

I don't know about that, Melinda said, but Jennifer only walked ahead of them, marching away like a child who had never heard the word no enough times, and there was nothing to do but to follow in her tracks. It didn't even matter about the silver lock on the door of the barn either, she only circled around, looking the wall up and down, her hands in her back pockets and determination set on her face, until finally she found the two loose boards in the back.

Come on, aren't you curious? she asked. Don't you have any sense of adventure? She kneeled to the ground and pushed the boards inward, just far enough to allow room for them to wriggle in one at a time. Stay out if you want to, she said, but I'm going in.

She lay down on her back and pushed her way through, and Wesley looked at Melinda. They didn't say anything but he knew they would follow. Inside the darkness was sliced into lines by sunlight cutting through the cracks and he watched the light on Jennifer's face. Her mouth dropped in awe as she looked at the long green buds dangling in neat rows from the chicken-wire ceiling like some exotic upside-down kind of crop. This is incredible, she said. This is unbelievable, thousands of dollars worth of dope, you could get high on it for years I'll bet. She walked in a slow circle beneath the buds, her mouth open and the slivers of light glancing off her white sweater.

Melinda said she'd seen enough already and started away backward and Wesley edged back with her but Jennifer was intent on taking down at least one long stemful. Who would miss it? she wanted to know, with all this wealth around everywhere. She reached up into the buds, her body stretching, the tilt of her against the dark, and she was just loosening a stem when the bang sounded outside, a closing door near the barn. Everyone froze, then the rattle of the lock and Melinda whispered, Hide, hide over here. She was already dodging toward a dark, empty stall, and Jennifer said, Why should we hide? It's your own father's place. And besides our cars are out there in plain view anyway.

Melinda and Wesley crouched down into the straw-scattered stall just the same, the splintery wall, the cool and damp, and Jennifer finally squeezed between them, the warmth of her pressed to Wesley's side, just as the door opened and the bare afternoon light spilled in on the floor.

At the door somebody coughed and then spit and a shadow lengthened in the pool of light, and on the far side of the barn, there it was, impossible to miss, where the loose boards slanted in, the other pool of light stretched out on the straw.

Well now, the voice at the door said and it was Roy Dale, Wesley could tell, and Well, well, what's going on here? Charlie, get my twenty-two out of the truck, I think we got us some rats in the barn again.

Oh shit, Jennifer whispered and Melinda said, Shhh.

Yessir, Roy said. The only thing to do with rats is to start firing away and watch the bastards go scurrying around. That's all you can do.

Jennifer looked at Wesley, her eyes wide and her bottom lip dropped, and he just said, Don't worry, he's not going to shoot anyone. He patted her leg and stood and walked to the edge of the light. It's just me, he said. I just came up to check around, and Roy Dale squinted and looked him over. Roy's eyebrow was split and knotted so that one eye was no more than a slit and his lip thickly swollen, cocking up his mustache like a bristled arrow pointing to the discolored cheek. Just you, huh? he asked. What'd you do, drive two cars out here today? I tell you what, I'd like to see that, someone that could drive two cars, wouldn't you, Charlie?

Charlie stood just behind him now and said that he sure hadn't ever seen anybody drive two cars at the same time before and didn't hardly see how it could be done, and then Melinda was next to Wesley. Hey Roy, she said.

Well, if it ain't the boss man's daughter, he said.

I just wanted to come and look at the old barn

where I used to play when I was little, she said. It was just for old times' sake, and Roy nodded, Uh-huh, uh-huh, and then Jennifer walked away from the shadows too and the lines of sarcasm fell away from his face.

Why didn't you say so, he said, his voice all warmth and good humor now. I'd of unlocked the door for you and showed you around myself. He walked in a half circle to his right, never taking his eyes away from Jennifer, and then stopped and nodded up toward the hanging buds. If anyone was interested he just wanted them to know that they were standing under the best dope in Oklahoma and he would guarantee it. He would stake his reputation on it and his reputation was as good as it got.

Jennifer stepped forward into the light and faced Roy Dale straight away, never letting on about the cuts and the bruises. She shaded her eyes against the incoming sun and How about proving it, she said. How about you let us make up our own minds about how good it is?

Roy smiled his hard cracked smile and looked down and then up. Maybe I can make a deal with you, he said. Maybe we can scratch each other's backs a little bit here. He removed his hat and rubbed back his hair. Here's the deal, something happened and we ended up with a extra share that we're gonna have to get rid of. The thing is it has to be cut up and bagged, so you help me make some money and I'll get you good and loaded. I'll get you loaded all the way up and then some.

Wesley started to say thanks but they weren't really interested in anything like that but Jennifer interrupted, glancing his way before turning back to Roy. What do we have to do? she said, and the smile on Roy's face twisted tighter. I like your attitude, he said, and she was right there by Wesley's side but the feeling came across him that she was too far away to even hear him if he spoke.

In the south parking lot of the high school the next morning, Melinda said it was crazy and she wouldn't go out there no matter how much money they got. She didn't care about the money and she could take or leave getting high and if they wanted to know the truth, Roy Dale gave her the creeps, even if he was seeing Wesley's mother.

Wesley sat at the steering wheel, a sinking feeling in his stomach. He knew he would cut school, he would have to, not for the money or any of that but because he couldn't let Jennifer go out there alone.

Go on if you want to but I'm going to class, Melinda said and stepped out of the car, so it was just the two of them then and as they drove out of town Jennifer talked happily about anything that came into her mind and Wesley only stared straight ahead. At Sam Casey's place, Roy took them out to the barn and

146

showed them how to cut down the marijuana buds for maximum profit. It was cool in the barn, though not so much for early November, and the double doors stood open, showing the view of the road and the field, the morning light spread upon it. They should have had all the dope clipped already, Roy explained, but the funeral had come up and everybody abandoned the crop and now he wanted to get enough ready to sell to a lawyer he knew up in Tulsa before Sam Casey returned.

Jennifer liked the work and caught on to it quickly and it was good to see her enjoy herself and the darkness in her gone. Wesley would look up from his heavy scissors and watch her intently clipping at the buds, and this was how it could be sometime in the future, her working beside him, planting flowers or something else normal like that, in front of a little white house in some other town. He could be an electrician like his own father was and maybe on Friday nights they would put aside time to do all the housework together and the place wouldn't be fancy or expensive but it would be clean and in a decent part of town. They would have their room in the very back and a living room with two leather couches and a little kitchen and another bedroom for Nelson. And if his mother wanted to live there, they'd have her too.

The barn began to warm up as they worked and the light grew more intense on the field outside. After a couple of hours Roy began to package the clippings in large plastic baggies. He weighed them with a small chrome scale and then fitted them into a special compartment he had fashioned under the seat of his truck. He said that if they came to Tulsa with him to meet with this lawyer, one of his regulars, they could smoke all they wanted and he'd pay them in cash when he got paid. That sounded good to Jennifer and Wesley said sure, as long as they got back in time for his gas station job.

Fuck the gas station, Roy said. You stick with me and you'll make ten times more money than you ever will at a goddamn gas station.

On the drive to Tulsa Jennifer sat in the middle and Roy passed down a marijuana cigarette and the smell of it hung thick inside the cab. The highway wound through the tall rounded hills and everywhere broomweed and blackjacks and the dry autumn brown heaped up to the sky. This is great dope, Jennifer said, I bet it's as good as anything the hippies had in the sixties, and Roy said, Shit, the dope they had in the sixties was dirtweed compared to this, compared to this all that old weed would do is give you a headache and the munchies, and that was all it took to get him started. He picked at the cut on his eyebrow and said the hippies were a bunch of addle-brained fools. They lived in a land of make-believe then. Take Sam Casey and his Sunshine People for instance, he said. Stupid

longhaired kids from all over the Southwest, thinking
they could go out and start up their own Garden of
Eden. It wasn't even the sixties anymore anyway, it was
seventy-two or seventy-three by then, too late for
that kind of fairy tale deal. Sam and Ansel and all their
Walden Pond shit and their Utopia delusions, they
were just lucky no Charles Manson showed up, they'd
have let him in trusting as hell and everybody would
have woke up murdered in their sleep. Sam and Ansel
and Joanne and Margaret and Beeline and all the others. If everybody would just do their share, Sam would
say. If everybody would just do their share, but everything was always coming apart the way things always
came apart anywhere because that's how the world was
and there wasn't any amount of all working together
that could keep the world from unraveling around you,
and shit what a farce, what a joke, those old Sunshine
People days were nothing but children's dreams one
long summer.

The lawyer had a motel room in Tulsa just off I-44.
Roy parked around back and went in while Wesley
and Jennifer waited outside. He's a character, Jennifer
said when he was gone, but he sure has good pot, and
she leaned into Wesley and put her head on his shoulder. They were parked by a trash bin and a thick sheet
of plastic stuck out of the top and flapped in the wind
beside them and the acrid smell of rotting food seeped

through the rolled up window. Soon Roy reappeared
with a cumbersome black suitcase and they loaded
the cellophane bricks of marijuana into it and Roy
told them to come on, they might as well see how it
was done.

The room was at the far end of the pale blue
hall, no one to see them along the way except for a
withered brown chambermaid hunched over her cart.
Roy banged out the code of three rapid knocks and
two more spaced out, the door opened and there was
the lawyer in a wrinkled gray suit. He looked to be
about thirty-five, his head overlarge for his body but
with a handsome anchorman face, an unlit cigar the
size of a half-wasted pencil clenched in his teeth. His
name was Colby and he shook hands all around, not
furtive or worried in the least, but loud and hearty in
an aggressive sort of way, patting Roy on the back,
running his eyes up and down as Jennifer passed into
the room. Everybody sit down, sit down, he said, take
a load off, how about a drink? How about a little Jack
Daniels?

Wesley passed on the drink but Jennifer and Roy
both accepted and the lawyer rattled around with the
glasses and ice while Roy opened the suitcase on the
flowered bedspread. The curtains were all pulled closed
but every light in the room was lit, a strange hazy halo
around them, a false light fit for the generic furniture
there, the end tables and bureau, the uncomfortable

straight-backed chairs and the bland paintings of
South Seas twilight bolted to the walls. Colby served
the drinks then pulled up a chair between the bed
and Jennifer and began to sort through the bricks of
marijuana, looking alternately at the cut buds and at
Jennifer, and Ah, this is wonderful stuff, wonderful
stuff, he said, poking his nose all the way into the clippings and inhaling deeply. Just smell it, he said and
held out a handful and she inhaled. Isn't that the best
smell? he said. Fragrant. Nothing better than fresh
dope by the suitcaseful. Nothing better in the world.

He pulled out a pipe from his suit jacket then
and discarding the little cigar, packed the pipe full
and smoked and then packed it again and handed it to
Jennifer, leaning in close to her, flicking the lighter and
watching her intently as she sucked on the end of the
black mouthpiece and even when she pulled it away
and the smoke rolled in loose coils away from her lips.

The pipe went around the room several times
and each time Wesley only pretended to inhale and
the lawyer talked and Jennifer laughed at all his small
jokes and innuendos. This was no time to lose concen-
tration, Wesley told himself. There was something
strange about being here in the company of grown
men like this, even though Colby and Roy Dale didn't
really seem like men, not like his father had been.
They had something missing in them.

The room grew hazier and more drinks were

fixed and finally Colby volunteered to pay for every-one's dinner. The afternoon was too good to waste on going back to work and why didn't they all just come along with him. It would be steaks and more drinks all on his credit card and don't worry about being under-age, he told Jennifer, looking straight into her eyes. It's under control.

Wesley spoke up then. He had his job to go to and couldn't be late, people depended on him and all like that, but Jennifer looked at him, her lip curling with a hint of disdain, and Call in, she told him. Call in and say your car broke down. What can they do?

Yeah, Roy said. That looks like what you're going to have to do, pardner, because I'm your ride and I'm sure not passing up a free steak, and he laughed at that and thought it sounded so good he said it again.

So then, Colby said, that's settled, and he looked at Jennifer. I guess if they're riding over together, that means you might as well ride with me, just so I don't get lonely, if you know what I mean.

The house was empty again and Nelson walked to Ragel's and when he got there he said his brother had let him off up the street. Uh-huh, Ragel said. Okay. But my dad'll give you a ride home later. You don't have to worry about that.

Ragel's sister Lejeune was learning how to play golf from one of her high-school friends and they thought that would be funny, so they went over to the athletic field at the technical college to watch her. They sat at the top of the hill looking down. Lejeune was a big girl and the club looked very small in her hands. I don't believe I ever saw a girl play golf before, Nelson said, and Ragel said oh yes, they even had a team over at the high school and OSU gave a scholarship out in it and that's why his sister wanted to learn how to play.

Her friend was good at it and could launch a ball all the way from the backstop past the persimmon tree by the wire fence. She was skinny and blond-headed and made him think she was almost dancing with the way that she moved. Who's that? Nelson asked as the girl swung her club around again and Ragel said it was his sister's friend Melinda.

She sure is something, Nelson said and Ragel said that she sure was and then shook his head sorrow-fully as his sister, in her fuzzy orange sweater, clubbed at the ground with the stiff little iron. I think she's going to dig up that whole field before she ever hits anything, he said and finally they gave up on her and walked over to the pond and sat down and watched the geese drift in their friendly clusters across the gray surface. After a while Nelson asked Ragel if he could ask him a question and Ragel said sure. Nelson thought for a moment and then said, Do you think it means you'll go bad if you don't have a father?

Ragel weighed the question, giving it the proper

respect, before saying no. He said, My cousin don't have one and he's okay. I don't think he likes it that way but he came out all right. He's in college now.

They were quiet then before Ragel finally asked how come Nelson had said his brother drove him over when he never really did. Nelson picked at the grass between his legs for a moment and then explained that he said it because he didn't want Ragel to get the wrong idea about what his family was like. It was just that they were busy all the time and now his mother had this man she was seeing and Wesley had some girl he wanted to go out with too so they didn't have time to be thinking about him all the time. But that's okay, he said, I can get along, I already learned how. I just don't want to turn out bad.

That'd be something, Ragel said. I don't know what it'd be like not having someone around the house all the time. There's always someone around my house. Sometimes I wish they'd leave me alone for a change.

Nelson picked up a pebble and tossed it into the pond. No you don't, he said. He looked down to find another pebble but didn't pick any up. A patch of dry dirt spread away from the grass near his hand and in the middle of it a trail of ants moved steadily around the loose structures of their village, their own pyramids, and watching them Nelson could only think of how one footfall would be like an atomic bomb coming down and still there the ants went in their winding lines, carrying their impossible boulders, just like the world could go on forever.

They were just starting back home when Nelson saw the figure on top of the hill on the parking lot side of the athletic field and at first he thought he was imagining it the way he sometimes imagined he saw the teenagers with the long hair and torn jeans, but the small engine cranked up and the crew-cut boy came bouncing down the yellow hillside toward them on the minibike. Come on, Nelson said, let's get out of here, but it was too late, the minibike was upon them and the boy circled around and stopped. He stood straddling the minibike, his hands clutching the handlebars, and Look, he said, it's the two little homos, the two little thimbledick queers.

You better get on out of here, Ragel said. He didn't step forward and he didn't step away. We aren't gonna take anything off you, so you might as well just go on, and Nelson stood close to his shoulder looking nowhere but at the boy's meaty fists on the handle grips.

The boy revved the throttle once and You know what? he said. I think I'll beat the shit out of you this time. I'll beat the shit out of you first and then I'll beat the shit out of your buddy again just for good measure.

You know what's the matter with you, Ragel said. People treat you like trash and so you have to go around treating other people like trash. My daddy told me about that, he told me all about what makes people like you.

The boy stepped off the bike now. You calling me trash, niggerboy, you calling me trash, and he was right in front of Ragel when Lejeune and her friend walked up. This boy giving you trouble here, Ragel? Lejeune said and she stood next to Nelson, planted her legs and put her hands on her hips, and Ragel said, I think he was thinking about it.

Shit, the boy said, stepping back. What do you think this water buffalo's gonna do? You think she's gonna help? I'm not afraid of any water buffalo.

Now, Lejeune said, craning her head around to look at her girlfriend. Huh-uh, she said. He didn't say what I think he said, did he? and her friend nodded and said, Uh-huh, he sure did, and that was all, Lejeune sprang into the crew-cut boy in a fluid motion belying her size, her big arms and legs churning and the boy twisting around, stumbling away from the minibike, bent at the waist, his back turned to her but his arms pumping behind him as though he could ward her off with backward punches, and she barreled into him until he was on the ground and she straddled his back, saying, Now I know you aren't gonna be bothering these boys anymore, are you. Are you? and slapped the back of his meaty head with the flat of her hand and he finally said, No, I don't guess I am.

You're not what? she said, her hand raised, and

156

No, I'm not gonna bother em anymore, he said, his voice cracking. I'm not ever gonna bother em anymore.

And you're not calling any more names anymore either now, are you? Her hand was poised in the air, and Huh-uh, he said. I'm not calling anybody any more names either, and that was it, she let him up and brushed the grass off herself, all the while watching him carefully as he picked up the minibike, handling it like some wounded thing, his head lowered, his eyes hidden, but Nelson could see the tear tracks on his cheeks, tear tracks stained with brown dirt, and when he rode away the whine of the engine sounded thin and weak and then faded into the air altogether.

Now, Lejeune said, clapping her broad hands together, it's getting chilly out here, you boys better come on home and have some dinner.

Nelson looked over his shoulder and the boy on the minibike was gone from view. Come on, Ragel said. You can eat with us and then my dad'll drive you home. He had already started walking and Nelson double-stepped to catch up. Lejeune and the girl named Melinda walked on ahead and he could picture himself among them, the whole family at the table and smiling all around, Lejeune on one side of him and Melinda on the other.

Maggie exhaled a cloud of cigarette smoke that filled the inside of the car and said, I'm glad you found somebody and all like that. I mean, I know I couldn't go as long as you did without sex, but I don't know about this Roy character. Now he doesn't even show up to drive you home from work like he said he was going to do. To me, he seems like all slick talk and a mean streak on top of that.

Donna looked out the windshield, the pickup trucks and rusted cars and the semi blowing out its diesel smoke and beyond that the cinder-block Dairy Queen and the Simple Simon's Pizza filling up with customers on their way home from work. You don't know him, she said. He's got another side to him too.

That's okay, Maggie said, but being good in bed isn't everything.

That's not what I'm talking about, Donna said. I mean, he's got more to him than he lets on, I think. He's spontaneous for one thing and I miss being that way. Just doing stuff without thinking about it so much. And besides I like the idea of that ranch he's got with his aunt. Did I ever tell you about how he wants to fix it to where kids could come out there in the summer, kids who've been abused or have family problems? And even if that doesn't come through, I like the idea of a place out in the country away from things. Sometimes I think I ought to just send the boys back to stay with my mother for a while, but maybe if we could get somewhere out in the country there wouldn't be so much to worry about.

Raise the kids out there with that Roy character? Maggie said. Are you serious? You'd be better off by yourself. Besides there isn't anyplace where you don't have to worry. You can't just keep moving from one place to another. I mean, look at you, you moved from the city to a small town to get away from things and now you want to move to the country. What are you gonna do after that, move into a hole in the ground?

All I want is a house again, Donna said, like the one me and Jack had. Not some run-down rent house. A real house with brick walls and storm windows. A place where you can't hear the wind coming through the walls.

Well, I'll tell you what. I wouldn't count too much on that ranch if I was you, not until he takes you out there to see it. For all you know he made the whole thing up. For all you know he could live in a halfway house up in Muskogee and has to break out every night just to see you.

Donna shook her head. He's going to take me up there. It's just that his aunt's got leukemia and can't have visitors around. But he's going to take me up there in a couple of weeks.

Maggie stubbed out her cigarette and said she would believe that when it happened, and Donna told her, Hey, he's sure a lot better than that lunatic you fixed me up with. At least he's not throwing me down on the parking lot.

Well, Maggie said. I'm sorry about that. But I
sure think you could do better than Roy. If you want to
know the truth I think you're seeing him because you
know he couldn't ever mean anything much to you.
That's what I think.

What's that supposed to mean?

You know what it means. You don't want to start
seeing someone and get all attached and have something go wrong again. But let me make a prediction for
you, one of these days you're going to meet up with
someone and you're not going to be able to keep from
getting involved no matter how hard you try.

Donna turned away. They were in the residential
section now and the lawns all looked gray. I don't know
about that, she said. If there's someone like that around
anymore, I sure don't know who it would be.

On his way back home from Ansel's, Sam turned the
curve and the place looked more empty even than
usual. At least the boy's car was parked out front and
he thought maybe Wesley would be there looking after
the quail, but even Charlie or Roy Dale would be better than no one right now. As he parked he noticed the
barn door standing slightly open and walked up to see
if maybe someone was around after all but instead
he found the spread tarp with the newly stripped stalks.
At first he thought, Good for Roy, good for him and
Charlie getting a start on things without having to be

told, but the clipped marijuana was nowhere to be found and he knew what Roy was thinking then.

He called Roy's Aunt Boots but she didn't know where he was and didn't care if he stayed away for good, so he drove by J. W.'s and Checkers and then thought of the boy and his mother. Her name and address were in the phone book and he drove down the graveled road looking for her house in the early darkness. At the end of the road he found a small, sagging house with numbers hanging loose and hard to decipher and he guessed he wasn't surprised it looked like that.

Roy Dale's truck wasn't there but Sam planned to be firm and find out from her just where he was, just what he thought he was doing, Ansel only gone a few days and his wife and kids left there without him, but then she came to the door in her white shirt and blue jeans and her brown hair hanging down to her shoulders and the first words to come to him were I'm sorry. I'm sorry to bother you, he said. He introduced himself and told how he worked with Roy Dale and needed to talk with him about something they were working on and he was just wondering if she knew where he was.

She smiled and opened the screen door. I'm glad to finally meet you, she said, stepping out onto the porch. I've heard a lot about you. Her eyes were very dark brown and her smile was the kind someone might put on at a funeral for the sake of being polite, and she was not what he had expected at all.

I've heard about you too, he said. Only, I don't know, you don't seem exactly like I thought you'd be.

Oh really? Why's that?

I don't know, you just seem different.

Like how?

Well, nothing against Roy or anything but you have a little more substance to you than the kind of women he usually goes out with.

Substance? What does that mean, I'm older?

No, nothing like that. I mean, you know, like someone you'd like to sit down and talk to for a while. Substance.

Roy doesn't usually like to talk to the women he goes out with?

Probably not a whole lot, no.

She looked away. I guess that doesn't surprise me too much.

I'll bet you like to go camping too.

I used to. She smiled. How'd you know that?

Sometimes I can tell things about people. It's just a knack I have.

She looked into his eyes for a second and then looked away as though something had frightened her. I hope you can't tell too much, she said.

No, I never can tell too much, he said. I can always tell just enough.

That made her smile again but she didn't look up. Well, I wish I could tell you where Roy was, she

162

said. But I haven't talked to him at all today. He can be kind of hard to get in touch with when he wants to.

I know, Sam said, he sure can be. He stood sideways on the porch now and looked at the road and there was no reason to stay, but he remained there watching the empty road, wondering what else to say, but he couldn't think of anything. Then just as he was about to turn away, she said, I'm sorry about your friend.

He looked back at her. Roy told me about him, she said. I sure hated to hear it. I know how it is to lose somebody like that. She seemed to be looking at something just over his shoulder.

Thanks, he said. You should've met him. Old Ansel. He was one of a kind, that's for sure.

Out in the dark, a car stopped in the road and it idled for a second, its headlights stretched above the gravel, before a little boy got out, a thin shadow that gained form as he walked up to the lit porch where they stood. Where have you been, young man, she said, her voice straining for authority and not quite making it there, and he told her he'd been at his friend's house for dinner and he tried to call but she wasn't there. She looked up at Sam then, embarrassed. Well okay, she said, turning back to the boy. But you need to let me know things like that ahead of time from now on, and the boy said that he would. She introduced him to Sam then and they shook hands. He looked up, a serious expression in his eyes, face very small and the remnants of a black eye, and Sam hadn't expected him either.

Well, I guess I'd better get going, Sam said.

All right, she said, If he comes by I'll tell him you were looking for him.

Sam stopped at the bottom of the steps. What?

Roy Dale, if he comes by I'll tell him you were looking for him.

Oh yeah, he said. Thanks, and before he started away again he said, You'll have to come out sometime and visit, and she said she would. She said she'd like that very much.

Are you jealous or something? Jennifer asked and Wesley said no he wasn't jealous, he just thought it was strange the way Colby gawked at her and asked her so many questions and besides she didn't have to ride over to that restaurant with him.

But he's a old man, she said, probably almost forty, and married with a daughter and everything. He showed me his wife's picture.

I just think it's strange, that's all, Wesley said. He opened the car door for her and when he got in on the other side she crawled across the seat saying, Well, let me show you something, I just want to show you one thing, and she kissed him, a hard open-mouthed kiss and her hands in his hair and then one down the front of his shirt and Don't start the car yet, she said. We don't have to go back for a while. Her kisses moved down his jaw and onto his neck and Wesley looked out the windshield to see if Roy Dale still lingered on the front yard and then her mouth was on his again and she straddled him, accidentally honking the horn as she moved over, her hands in his hair and then her fingers on his chest and undoing the buttons on his shirt, her touch cold at first against his skin. God, I wish we had a motel room, she said. I wish we had a motel room like that one Colby had, don't you? But her mouth was back on his before he could answer and she moved up and his lips were against her neck, softness and heat and the smell of her body barely beneath her perfume and shampoo, her breath in his ear and wet kisses and the movement of her heaving against him like a wave on the verge of sweeping him down, and she rose higher and now took her hands away, unsnapped her pants and the zipper came open like a flower blooming all at once, but he said, Don't. He said, Don't, and put his hand over hers and stopped her and sat back in the seat, feeling as though he had thrust up through the surface of the ocean just before drowning. Slow down, he said. You had too much to drink, but she just nuzzled her hair into his eyes. Drinking makes me so horny, she said and licked the side of his face.

He grabbed her wrists and tilted his head so that

he could look into her eyes and Look, he told her, I'm not gonna take advantage of you like this.

You're not taking advantage of me, she said, her smile playful and sleepy both. I'm the one taking advantage of you, but he looked into her eyes and measured out what he wanted to say. I don't want it to be just some little game, he told her. I don't want it to be the kind of thing that a month from now we can't even remember how it happened.

She stared at him, her eyes half-closed, the smile unraveling.

Okay? he said.

Okay, she whispered and collapsed into him, then down in the seat, deflated and silent, like somebody crying only on the inside.

He drove her home then and outside her large white house, he leaned over and kissed her and her lips were gentle now. I had fun, she said sleepily, let's do it again.

We'll do something better next time, he said. I think I could think of something better to do than getting dragged along on a dope-selling deal.

I thought it was fun, she said and he told her that may be but it could also get her in a lot of trouble and he didn't want to see her in a lot of trouble.

I don't want to see you get in any trouble either, she said, touching the side of his face. I just want good good things for you.

No more dope selling then?

She closed her eyes and shook her head. No more, she said. No more.

Good. He brushed back her hair and said he hoped her parents didn't notice she'd been drinking.

She looked away toward the house. They won't notice a thing, she said. They won't even notice I'm home.

When she got out, he watched her start up the flagstone walk and in the middle of it she skipped a couple of times and then looked back at him and laughed.

Roy Dale stooped over in the little halo of light and began to roll up the tarp and Sam said, I guess you didn't think I'd get back this early.

At first Roy jumped at the sound but he composed himself and smiled a little half smile that only made the swollen lip seem more alien. Hey there boss, he said, how'd things go in Wichita Falls?

You could've seen how things went for yourself, Sam said, stepping into the light.

Roy cocked his head and Now, you know we talked about that, he said. I hadn't kept in touch with old Ansel like you did. And besides who was going to look after the place?

Sam studied the half-rolled tarp. Yeah, it appears

like you've been looking after things all right. What'd you do with it?

What'd I do with what?

You know.

Roy adjusted his cap self-consciously and said, I took a trip up to see Colby.

Sam walked closer and stopped within arm's reach of Roy. I hope you don't have any ideas about keeping Ansel's share, he said.

Now wait a minute, Roy said. I thought the rule was if anybody didn't put in their part of the work, then that was it, they gave up their share.

Ansel put in his damn share of the work, Sam said, his fists tightening at his sides. He put in more than his share of the work and you know it. There wasn't anything about dying in the rules. That wasn't anything anybody even thought of.

I don't know, Sam, Roy said. I sure didn't see Ansel up here that much last summer like me and Charlie were.

Shut up, Roy, Sam said. Just shut up. Ansel's share's going to his wife and kids. I don't care who has to sell it. They're getting his share and that's all there is to it. And if you had any kind of heart you'd kick in a little extra to go with it too.

Hell, Roy muttered, looking down, Ansel's damn kids didn't ever even step foot on the place, but Sam just turned and said, I'm not going to talk to you any-more about it. This is still my place and I'll expect Colby's money on my kitchen table tomorrow morn-ing. I'll split it up just like we've always done. Behind him, Roy was still muttering but Sam continued on outside and turned the corner and headed up through the dark to the empty house.

Roy had planned to go to bed early that night after all the smoking and drinking he had done in the afternoon but now he changed his mind. He picked up Charlie and they stopped for a six-pack and headed for J. W.'s. Charlie wanted to know why Roy hadn't taken him along to Tulsa. I sure would of liked to of had me a steak too, he said but Roy just said forget about that, it wouldn't have worked.

Why not? Charlie said. I've been other times on things like that.

Well hell, Roy said. If you're gonna keep bugging me, I'll tell you. I didn't take you along because you would of fucked it up. This guy's a lawyer, he's a smart guy and doesn't want some big dumb ass along. There, that's it, are you satisfied?

Charlie turned and stared out the windshield. Well shit, he said. Shit. They continued on and Roy made the turn at the abandoned factory. That's a hell of a thing, Charlie said finally. Calling me a dumb ass and all like that. I could of talked to a damn lawyer. I talked to your lawyer that time, remember? Me and him got along good too.

Hell Charlie, it's the same guy, Roy said. It's the same damn lawyer. That's what I'm talking about, saying dumb things like that. You'd make him nervous.

Well, you never said he was the same lawyer, Charlie said and Roy looked at him then and thought that he might be on the verge of tears. Just forget it, Charlie, he said. I'll take you next time. Shit.

It was nearing midnight when they pulled into the parking lot at J. W.'s and parked in the back corner under the naked branches of the oak tree there. Roy recognized a couple of the cars, a weathered station wagon and a rebuilt Chevy Nova. He turned off the engine and the headlights and leaned back in his seat and studied the Nova, the hood scoop, the jacked-up rear, the newly applied gray primer waiting for the final coat of paint.

You know what? he said after a while. I'm not gonna kick his ass. Hell no. He'd get over that too quick.

Who? Charlie asked and Roy only pointed to the knot on his eyebrow and Charlie said, Oh.

I'll bet he expects me to go in there, Roy said. Probably even has more of his buddies with him this time, but fuck it, I'm not going in there. Not yet anyways.

He finished off his beer, stepped out of the

truck, crossed the lot to the Nova and circled around it, sizing up the work that had been done, the care and perseverance and commitment, the long hours, the pride, a person's whole identity went into work like that, and he stopped by the driver's side window and stood staring at it, his own shadow in the glass, and then with one foot planted he rocked back and kicked the window as hard as he could and then again and again but the glass wouldn't break. Sonofabitch, he said. Motherfucking sonofabitch. He stopped and walked away, then turned back and kicked again but this time lost his footing and landed on his back in the gravel. Goddamn that sonofabitch is tough, he said and on the other side of the car a methodical pounding started up, whump, whump, whump, Charlie punching the passenger window with his fist, over and over, whump, whump, and Hell now, Charlie, Roy said, standing up. You're gonna break your damn hand, but Charlie went on, his eyes focused only on the glass, his fist pumping like a piston, and whump, whump, until finally the glass exploded inward and his fist with it, glass inside on the restored seats and down in the gravel and a stream of blood all down his arm as Roy came around and grabbed him. Ah shit now, Roy said. Look at that, you fucked up your hand. What'd you do that for?

Charlie looked at his bleeding hand almost as though it belonged to somebody else and That motherfucker, he said, that motherfucker, I'd bust his ass, I'd bust his ass just like this window. Fried out sonofabitch don't know who he's dealing with when he fucks with us. Sonofabitch, and Roy pulled him away and led him to the truck, saying, Save it, Charlie. Save that shit for when we need it.

They drove back down the dark road and past the abandoned warehouse and the shotgun shacks and the refinery, both of them silent, Charlie dousing the cut on his hand with beer and Roy taking deep gulps, and they had almost reached home before Roy said anything. He didn't look at Charlie but stayed turned to the windshield and I didn't mean that, he said. You know, about you being a dumb ass. I was just pissed off is all. Damn Sam Casey and that bastard with the Nova and all that. Next trip up to see Colby, I'll bring you along.

Aw, that's all right, Charlie said. Roy looked at him now and he was smiling.

How's that hand? Roy asked and Charlie said that he guessed he'd live.

Sure you will, Roy told him. I wouldn't let anything happen to you.

Nelson told Wesley how they had pancakes and sausage and bacon for dinner, Ragel's family, breakfast right there at dinner, pancakes and sausage and bacon and scrambled eggs with Louisiana hot sauce on top, and all of them around the dinner table with Ragel's father at one end starting the prayer and his mother right next to him passing around dishes, and you should have seen Lejeune, she had everybody laughing from the time they sat down. She told a joke about God and the accumulation of money and her father said not to tell jokes that had God in them but he laughed at her anyway just like everybody did because you couldn't help it with her, and Jevon and Donnel and Toymeka were there, and a girl named Melinda, everybody saying how their day went and Nelson even said how his went too with the whole family listening.

Wesley said he knew Melinda from school, if this was the same one. She's real nice, he said, never looking down or slowing his walk as he headed to the car.

I'll bet you all had a good time. Now I'll be seeing you, I've got to take Jennifer out to her cousin's before I go into work.

Nelson stopped in the middle of the yard and watched Wesley go. I wish I lived over there with them, he said almost to himself. I'd always have somebody to do something with then.

Wesley stopped then and turned around. Don't say that kind of thing. What if Mama heard you talking that way? He looked away and then back. I'll tell you what, what are you doing right now?

I'm not doing anything.

Then why don't you come along with us. She's gonna pick up a puppy and maybe you can play with it some.

Are you sure she won't get mad? Nelson asked and Wesley said that he was. He said she would be glad to have him along but he didn't sound all the way certain about it being true.

They picked her up at a big white house with a wide sloping lawn and when she came out Melinda was with her. Jennifer sat in the front and Melinda sat in the back with Nelson. She asked how he was and smiled and shook his hand, all very adultlike, her eyelashes so light you could see right through them, her eyes pale blue, like the color of the ocean on the maps at school. I didn't know you were Wesley's little brother, she said. But I guess you don't talk a whole lot.

He can be kind of shy, Wesley said and Nelson said not all the time he wasn't, but sometimes he just liked to listen.

Well, that's a good way to be, Melinda said, but Jennifer looked at Wesley and said, Why'd you bring him along with us?

Because he's my brother, Wesley said and that was all he said about it and she just crossed her arms and stared away out the window.

They passed out of town into the country, the yellow grass high along the side of the road, the scrub oaks gaunt, nearly leafless against the gray-blue wall of the sky. Nelson tried sneaking a glance over at Melinda again but she caught him and said, What? He didn't know what to say back though and turned away red faced and looked straight ahead.

After a while Jennifer warmed up and moved close to Wesley again, her head leaned toward his shoulder but not touching and he asked her about Thursday and where she had been. She just had some things to do, she told him, leaning back away. Me and my sister, we went up to Tulsa to get her some basketball shoes, that's all.

Wesley asked why she didn't just get them at Gorshin's in town and she went on about how they never had the right kind and then turning to the window again said, There's the creek where we used to go skinny-dipping when I was in grade school, but there

175

was something false in her voice and Nelson wondered if Wesley heard it there too.

Her cousin's place was a trailer house stuck back in the brush like a discarded tin can, rust stained and crumpled, the yellow grass shaggy around it, two mis-shapen pickups on the wide gravel drive, and a warped wooden porch added on to the front with two rifles leaning against the wall. Wesley and Jennifer got out but Melinda said she'd wait with Nelson, and maybe they would take a walk around the woods to see what was there. Wesley said he wouldn't be gone long, and he and Jennifer walked up to the trailer and waited on the porch next to the rifles. Nelson studied the two of them, Wesley leaning toward her and Jennifer leaning toward the door. She reached out and knocked, her brown hair hanging long down the side of her face, like a curtain she'd drawn to hide her true self, and Nelson wondered why it was that Wesley couldn't see through it.

Jennifer's cousin was in his early twenties, tall and muscled-up through the chest, and he wore black-framed glasses and a camouflage cap, a ponytail hang-ing down from the back. He led them into the living room where an open tool chest sat on the floor next to a plastic laundry basket, and screwdrivers and wrenches lay side by side with wadded-up jeans and T-shirts. A cheap stereo was arranged on a set of shelves constructed of unvarnished wood planks and on the wall behind it hung a ragged Confederate flag. Among all of the clutter, in a gold crushed-velvet chair at the far end of the coffee table, sat a slightly older man, twenty-four or twenty-five, also in camouflage, with a full black beard that covered the bottom of his face like a mask. A pistol and a marijuana pipe and a few crumbled stems lay on the table before him and Wesley thought maybe they weren't just here for a puppy after all.

He and Jennifer sat on the sofa next to her cousin. His name was Mike and the man in the chair was Lawrence but whether it was his first name or last never was told. So do you have it? Mike asked and Jennifer tapped her purse and told him, Right here.

I'm not buying anything without trying it first, Lawrence said from the depths of the crushed-velvet chair, his voice flat and his mouth barely visible behind the thick black beard even when he spoke. Jennifer told him she figured on that, she never expected anything else, and pulled the plastic baggy out from her purse.

Where did you get that? Wesley asked, and looking down at the bag she said only that he knew where she got it, then opened the top and took the pipe from her cousin.

When did you go over there? Wesley watched as she tamped a pinch of marijuana into the bowl of the pipe and she told him she had got it just the other day,

Thursday, on the way to Tulsa. She had just stopped by because she knew her cousin wanted some and all like that. I know what you're thinking, she said, looking up from the pipe. You're thinking how I said I wasn't going to get involved in selling this stuff anymore.

That's pretty much what I remember you saying all right, Wesley said.

I know I did but wait till you see this puppy. It's a purebred and they've got papers on it and everything, there wasn't any way I could afford a purebred puppy like that. She had something close to a pleading look in her eyes.

So you're just going to make a trade for this puppy and that's it, huh?

That's it. I swear.

Jesus, Lawrence said, shaking his head. What do you got to explain yourself for? Is he your boyfriend or your daddy? Shit.

Hey, Jennifer said. He's just someone who cares what happens to me. How about that? Is that okay with you?

Lawrence looked away. Whatever makes your boat float.

All right then, she said.

The pipe went around, Mike first and then Lawrence and back to Jennifer, and Wesley only looked on, thinking how Jennifer trusted too much in the world to be safe. She thought she could come and go any place she wanted to and it would be a hard thing to show her that it wasn't true.

On the third round she had barely inhaled before bursting into a flurry of coughs and Mike and Lawrence started laughing. When she had composed herself she said, Now you're not going to tell me this isn't some pretty good stuff. They agreed that it was but Lawrence said that just to make sure to load them all up another round. Pretty good was all right, he said, but for a rottweiler pup it better be damn good stuff.

The football was underinflated and soft from lying unused on the back floorboard of the car but that only made it easier to catch and Nelson couldn't believe a girl could throw as hard as Melinda. He ran through the high grass in front of the trailer and the ball flew overhead, perfectly spiraled, like a thing propelled on its own, so far he couldn't reach it and it spattered in the gravel and bounded away into the rim of the woods. Sorry, she called and he said, That's okay. That was some kind of pass.

Beyond the tree line the grass rose higher and brown crackled vines looped down and jagged brown stones littered the ground, collecting fallen leaves around them, and just beyond where the football lay couched in a pocket of grass, a muscular black dog pawed at the earth, intent on his work until Nelson's footsteps startled him. His head jerked up and his muscles coiled and That's all right, Nelson said, freezing where he stood. That's all right, boy. But the dog stood his ground, a low growl starting in his throat, his eyes cut with some deep hurt that had collected meanness around it like scar tissue. The growl swelled louder, and Nobody's gonna hurt you, Nelson said. Nobody's gonna hurt you.

The dog looked ready to lunge forward at any second but then Melinda was there and told Nelson don't move. She stepped up and threw a rock into the dirt just in front of the dog and he flinched and moved one step away, half-turned, and she threw another rock, closer this time. Go on, she said. Get out of here. There's nothing for you here, and the dog edged back, his ears laid close to his head, until the third rock hit the ground between his legs. He turned and trotted into the grass, turning back only once. Then he was gone and only the feeling of menace left in the hollow where he'd been.

He was a big one, Nelson said, looking up at Melinda and she said he sure was. Nelson picked up the football and they headed back. Do you think he could of killed somebody? he asked but she said that she didn't think so. She figured maybe he could kill a rabbit or something but that was all, and Nelson shook his head and said that would be bad enough because you never knew but what a rabbit might have his own family back somewhere in a hole under a tree waiting for him to come home, only he never would.

So where's my puppy? Jennifer said and Mike told her it was out back and he'd go get it.

Make sure and close that gate out there so the dog don't get out again, Lawrence said and then flicked the lighter over the pipe another time. When Mike was gone, he picked up the pistol from the table, spun the cylinder around and casually aimed at the lamp near the window.

That's some kind of beard you got there, Jennifer said and he looked at her and smiled, though it was hard to tell. It makes you look like a mountain man, she said.

He held the pistol back by his ear, barrel up. That's because that's what I am, he said.

You're kind of far away from the mountains, aren't you? Wesley hadn't meant to sound sarcastic but Lawrence never looked at him, he only stared hard at Jennifer and said, What I'm talking about is a way of life. He looked at his pistol, touched his finger to his tongue and dabbed at a smudge on the barrel. I'm talking about survival of the fittest and making damn sure I'm the fittest there is for when the niggers revolt.

I didn't know they were going to, Jennifer said and Wesley said, They aren't.

Lawrence looked at Wesley then. Anybody on

181

the nigger's side might as well be one too, he said, and I'd shoot a white nigger as soon as a black one, it doesn't make any difference to me.

What are you, in one of those white supremacist groups or something like that? Wesley asked and Lawrence narrowed his eyes and said, I might be and I might not.

Just then Mike returned carrying a black rottweiler puppy and Jennifer's face lit up. Oh, look at you, she said. Look at you, aren't you the most precious thing. You are precious, aren't you?

Sonofabitch'll be a killer when he grows up, Mike said, hoisting the puppy into her hands. She held the dog up, its large black paws kicking the air, and touched its nose with hers. You're a big boy, she said in a baby voice. You're Mama's big boy. Yes you are.

Wesley leaned over and patted the dog's head. Wait till Nelson sees that, he said. He'll think that's really something. Jennifer lowered the dog and her baby voice was gone. Well, if he's real careful, she said, I'll let him hold him for a while. The smell of the dog was strong in the air now and she hugged the squirming body to her chest, the baby voice back, and We have to be careful with you, don't we? she said. We have to take good care of you. Yes we do. Yes we do.

She's gonna spoil that dog, Lawrence said. He'll get all soft and not good for a good goddamn.

182

He won't care, she said. He's gonna like getting spoiled.

He won't like it when some other dog comes along and chews out his damn jugular, I'll tell you that for sure, and you won't like it too much when they're shoveling dirt over him either.

She lowered the dog into her lap and there was no remnant of the little girl voice anymore. Well, I'll tell you what, if I was a dog I'd sure rather have them throwing dirt down on me than belong to someone who kept me chained up out on some dry patch under a dead tree in the back yard. I'd rather them just shoot me the first day.

Hey, Lawrence said, that could be arranged too pretty easy, and he pointed the pistol out, straight toward Jennifer's face. We could just shoot you now and bury you out in the woods and no one would even be able to identify your little old half-rotted body by the time they got you dug up.

Go on then, she said leaning her face forward over the dog's head, staring straight into the gun barrel. If you're man enough to do it, just go on. You think I even care? Go on.

Lawrence smiled but only in his eyes and Wesley stood and moved between Jennifer and him. Why don't you put that pistol down, he said, looking down into Lawrence's face. It isn't funny. He planted his feet and clenched his fists at his sides.

Lawrence held the revolver where it was for a moment but Wesley stood his ground. Hell, I was only joking, Lawrence said, leaning back in the chair and laying the gun down in his lap. Thing isn't even loaded. Damn girl here's got a screw loose though it looks like to me.

That was fun, Jennifer said. Maybe we can play Russian roulette next time I come over. She propped her chin on the puppy's head and gazed up at Wesley and smiled.

Nelson and Melinda walked along the narrow gravel driveway, and down near the roadside she sat on a cut stump and he sat in the grass next to her. She said she would teach him to play license-tag poker if any cars came by and they talked for a while until finally a car passed and she said, See there, that tag's got two threes. That's a pair. That'll be my hand and the next one will be yours. They talked some more and Nelson asked her if she had a boyfriend and she said no she didn't and he asked her how come. You're a lot better than that Jennifer girl ever thought about being, he told her.

She smiled at that and looked at the road. Jennifer's all right, she said. And she needs someone like Wesley. I think he'll be good for her.

I just hope she doesn't mess things up.

Don't worry about that. They might be right for each other and they might not be, but Wesley's always

184

going to be your brother. No matter what, that's not going to change.

Nelson thought about that. How does anybody know whether they're right for each other or not? he asked.

She considered the question for a moment, her lips pressing together, her eyes narrowing. Finally she said that she didn't know if you ever really could know it for sure. She said one time her parents thought they were the right ones for each other and now they hardly ever talked anymore and her mother was married to somebody else. He was okay, he wasn't mean or anything like that, but he was just kind of there, and not like her father at all. Not like her father used to be when they were a family living out in the country and sometimes even rode through the fields on the tractor together, and she still loved him but anymore he shut himself off in that empty farmhouse, hardly talking to anybody at all, and she wondered if he would ever find someone to bring him back out again, someone who'd stick by him this time. I guess that's what you really need to find, she said, just someone who won't ever give up on you when things get weird.

My dad was like that, Nelson said, looking down between his knees at the grass blades among the gravel. My mom used to be too back then. She said they were made for each other right to a tee but I guess something like that only happens once.

They both watched the road then and finally another car passed. The license tag had two eights and Melinda said, I guess you win. What do I owe you?

Nelson thought for a moment then said, I haven't been out on a farm before, that's something I'd sure like to see, and she said, All right then, that sounds fair enough to me. You just name the time and we'll go out to my dad's place.

They started back up the driveway then and when they reached the car, Wesley and Jennifer were already standing there and he was looking at her the way he sometimes did at their mother when she'd had too much to drink. I don't think you oughta come back out here, he told her. I don't think we oughta get involved with these kinds a guys, and she said, That's okay, I won't need to come out here anymore, now that I got my baby here. She had a black puppy nuzzled to her cheek, a smaller replica of the dog in the woods, and she turned and talked to it in a little girl voice that even the puppy tried to squirm away from.

When the winter cold came on it came all in one day the way it does and Sam Casey in his coat with the lamb's wool collar stood watching puffs of breath blow away from his front porch and he surveyed the land lying silent and frozen beyond. The quail were all gone from the pen next to the house, sold to restaurants and landowners for hunting leases, and nothing left to do now but prepare things for the cold months ahead.

He walked the perimeter of the pen and then out along the tree line and something drew him into the woods and down the narrow trail through the naked branches and dead stalks, the rivers of dry leaves running in gullies beside him, and all the way out to the marijuana field, where the tough jungle spread, gnarled and hard husks abandoned under the flat gray sky.

He had thought he could never come back here and now that he had he felt even more severed and if marijuana grew next year it would have to grow on its own with no help from him. Let whoever wanted to come harvest come, he wouldn't be with them, and let the seasons change and change again, he could never find promise here the way he had in the summers and falls of that other lifetime he had lived in that other age. He didn't know what else he would do but he would have to find something and when he turned his back on the field and started into the forest again he didn't think of the harvest or the Sunshine People or even Ansel but let his mind wander ahead of him and the woman was different than he could ever have expected, and her brown hair lay on the white shoulders of her shirt, and the distance in her eyes, a pain that seemed not so much for herself as the world and the way it was, and the boy, too, with the little cowlick on top and that grave way of looking up at you like he could see who you used to be.

Roy Dale told Donna the dope-selling game was a job like anything else, you packed up your samples and made your calls and took your cut of the commission like all salesmen did. And anyway it was only temporary until he raised enough money to invest in the ranch and on top of that smoking dope had never hurt him or anyone else. It doesn't seem to be hurting you any either, he told her.

Donna inhaled from the marijuana cigarette and then let out the smoke and the windshield fogged a little in front of her. It was cold in the truck and the heater only blew a dank, tepid air that didn't help very much. And so, she said, how long has Sam Casey been doing it, selling dope and that kind of thing? She asked the question casually, as though the answer didn't mean anything to her at all, and Roy said that Sam had been at it for a long time now, longer than anyone he knew, more than twenty years, and he might like to talk about selling quail or raising lima beans but he wouldn't, he wouldn't ever do anything else.

I don't know, Donna said. Sometimes people change. She pictured Sam Casey again, the way she had done since seeing him on her front porch that night, standing there half-turned, like a door that was just opening in front of her. Several times she had come close to calling him. She would just ask him how Wesley was doing with his part-time job out there and if that led to anything else then she would just see what happened. She never did though, she always stopped because of Roy, even though she suspected he wouldn't care all that much if he lost her, and maybe Maggie was right after all, she thought, maybe she was just afraid to let someone inside again after what had happened before, and of course Maggie was right, of course she was, it was the most obvious thing in the world.

But this ranch I'm building up is gonna be something, Roy said. We're gonna have Arabian horses. Did

I tell you that? Arabian fucking horses. I'm just a little bit worried about living out there right now, what with my Aunt having tuberculosis and all.

Tuberculosis? Donna said. I thought it was leukemia.

Roy said that was what he meant, he meant leukemia, and anyway he was worried about living there with her until she got better and he was just thinking that maybe he could come stay with Donna for a while.

She turned toward the side window of the truck and took a drink from her green glass and studied the dark for a second. I don't know, she said. I don't know about that. I've got the boys to think of, you know.

What does that mean? Do you think I'd be some kind of bad influence on them or something?

She kept looking out the window and all she would say was I don't know. I'll have to think about that.

Well, why don't you think about this while you're at it, I'm sure not any worse of a influence on them than you and your bottle of rum. What do you think the Human Services people would have to say about that shit? Hell, if you had any sense, you'd farm those boys out to your mother for a while like we talked about.

She looked back at him then and only paused a second. You might as well just tell me to kill myself, she said, staring into the hard lines of his face. Because

if I gave up those kids that'd be the end of me right
there and I know that for sure.

On the table candles flickered in their brass holders
and the wine glasses were filled up to the brim with
red wine. A white tablecloth and the pizza box already opened. Jennifer said her parents wouldn't
be back until long after midnight. She knew how
they were.

This is a great room, Wesley said, looking around
at the the dark wooden trim on the wall, the giant ar-
moire and the glass-covered still-life pictures. The
table itself was huge with heavy legs and high-backed
chairs gathered around as though waiting for more
important guests to arrive.

It's all right, Jennifer said. Most of the time I eat
up in my room watching TV. How about a couple of
appetizers? She pulled out a small prescription pill
bottle. They're just Ativans. My mom's.

I don't think so.

Come on, the only thing they do is relax you up
a little bit.

That's all right. I'm relaxed enough as it is.

Okay, she said. Then I guess I won't have any
either if you're not. She took the bottle back to the
kitchen, the sound of the pantry closing, and then she
was back. I guess you're going to save me from myself
yet, she said as she sat down.

Well, that'd be all right, wouldn't it?

She grinned. I don't know, I don't know if I want saving.

Everybody wants saving.

Maybe so, she said. She edged her chair close beside him so that they took up only one small corner of the table and then held up her wine glass. Here's to saving each other, she said and they clinked their glasses together.

They started on the pizza then and talked and he tried to find out more about her family and what they were like but she only gave the briefest of thumbnail sketches. Sometimes he could barely tell where the sarcasm left off and the truth took up but it kept coming around that her parents left her to herself most of the time and it had been that way for as long as she could remember.

And so what about you? she asked, winding a string of cheese away from the pizza with her finger. What's the big tragedy of your past that you don't like to talk about?

I told you about that, he said.

You told me what happened but you never really said what it was like.

What it was like?

She leaned toward him. I mean, you know, did you ever feel like you just wanted to die yourself after going through all that?

No, I never felt like I wanted to die, he said, setting the crust of pizza down. I still had my mother and my brother to think about. Maybe I felt like I wanted to kill somebody for a while though. For a pretty long time I felt like that. But I never felt like I wanted to die. I guess maybe my mother did though. Sometimes I think she still does.

Did she do something, try to kill herself or something?

Not the way you might think, not all at once. Maybe a little bit at a time.

She looked down at her plate. What do you mean, like by drinking and all?

I don't know, it's just the way she used to be and she isn't anymore. He picked up his napkin and wiped off his hands. Like when I was a kid I couldn't even complain about her to my friends when I'd get grounded or something because they all liked her so much. They'd say, What are you complaining about, your mother's so cool, and all like that. They'd say, I wish I had your mother. But she's not like that anymore.

He took another drink of the wine and stared at the candle for a moment. What about you? he said finally. What about your past?

She finished off her wine and reached for the bottle. I don't want to talk about the past anymore, she said. Too depressing. Let's talk about the future. A sly smile crossed her face and her eyebrows raised. Have you ever asked questions on a Ouija board?

He told her he hadn't and she pushed her plate away and said to wait right where he was, she had one upstairs. She brought it down and placed it on the table next to one of the candles. It really works, she said, rubbing her hands together over the board. I ask it questions all the time.

The board was light brown, a simulated wood color, with black letters and numbers and pictures of the sun and the moon, people and ghosts. On it lay a plastic pointer she called the oracle and she explained how they should just touch their fingers lightly to it and then ask a question and the oracle would point out the answer.

I'll ask it one first, she said. All the lights were off and the candlelight flickered on her face like a scene in some ghost story movie. What'll I ask it, she said. What'll I ask it. I know. Is this going to be the night? That's our first question. Is this going to be the night.

She shifted in her chair and smiled the sly smile again. Now close your eyes, she instructed, and put your fingers just right here on the side of the oracle and ask the question over and over in your mind, don't think about anything else, just that one thing or it won't work.

He closed his eyes and thought of that question, Is this going to be the night? Is this going to be the night? and he wasn't sure but he thought he felt the oracle move and the more he repeated the question the closer to Jennifer he felt, knowing that she was asking the same question in her mind too and that they both wanted the same answer.

Finally she said she felt it stop and to open their eyes and he looked down to see the oracle pointing to the word yes up in the corner next to the sun. Yes, she said and tickled the tops of his fingers with hers. And you know the Ouija board doesn't lie.

It doesn't?

No.

He looked down at the black letters arching across the board. Then maybe we ought to see how far into the future it goes.

It can go all the way to the end of the world if you want it to.

He looked back up and into her eyes. Then how about this, how about we ask it if we're always going to be together?

Always? she said, her eyes glancing down.

If it goes to the end of the world then it ought to know that.

I guess, she said. She straightened in her chair and they placed their fingers back on the edge of the oracle. He closed his eyes again and started the question, over and over. This time he wasn't so sure they both wanted the same answer but he never opened his eyes until she said it was time and then he looked down and the oracle had moved to the bottom of the board and pointed toward where it said good-bye.

Good-bye? he said. What does that mean?

I don't know, she said. Sometimes it likes to be mysterious, just out of meanness I think.

They reached Tulsa around eight and Roy's first call was at a half-dilapidated brick building with a tin real-estate sign leaning in the grass out front, a look of despair about it, as though it had abandoned hope of attracting any takers. Inside, the stairway was dark with haunted-house creaks and the odor of rancid meat and Donna said maybe she would go ahead and wait in the truck, but Roy said he didn't think that was such a good idea, not in this neighborhood it wasn't.

His first customer, he said, was a man named William William, just like that, both names the same, and he took a long time coming to the door. A whole series of locks, dead bolts and chains, clicked and rat-tled before the door finally opened and he led them in with the scurrying gait of some ground-dwelling ani-mal, hunched and furtive, his head oblong and com-pletely bald so that the folds at the base of his skull seemed like a toothless grimace misplaced there. The room was dank and cavelike, the tweed sofa and chair all threadbare and stained, the posters of the Beatles faded to lavender and barely discernible at all among

the shadows, and during the whole transaction, when
he wasn't checking through the metal blinds for the
FBI or the Weathermen, either one, all he wanted to
know was where was Sam Casey and when was he
coming? He could trust Sam, Sam was a good man,
the best, the best, his words all coming in short excited
bursts, and he was downcast almost to the point of
tears when Roy said that Sam hardly ever worked sales
himself anymore and maybe he did cry some when he
heard about Ansel and mumbled something about the
good dying young. Donna almost started to like him
but then his small eyes darted toward her and What's
she doing here? he wanted to know. Nothing had ever
happened to Ansel before she came around, and it was
all Roy could do to change the subject back to marijuana and money. Goddamn, William William said,
goddamn the inner machinery of the world, and then
he brought out his money in a paper grocery sack and
Roy traded him the cellophane bricks of marijuana
and Donna couldn't wait to get back to the truck and
her rum and Coke.

Let's go home, she said, this is too weird for me,
but Roy said no, there were more calls to make and he
was going to make them all.

Jennifer said, Wouldn't you like to be able to fly? If I
could fly I'd take off over all these rooftops and never
come back here. The two of them wrapped in a yellow

197

blanket, they sat on the peak of the roof that extended out next to her gabled window. She took a pull on her marijuana cigarette and then held it out to him but he waved it away.

You know what? she said. When you don't smoke pot with me it makes me feel separated off from you. I'm stoned and you're not. It makes me think you're thinking things about me.

Then don't smoke it, he said.

She looked at him for a second, her mouth hanging open. You don't want me to quit doing everything fun, do you?

No, but I'm just saying I don't want any.

I don't see how you can stand it, she said. Everything's so boring all the time around here but all you have to do is smoke a little of this and it makes it to where you can see the world like a little kid again.

I don't want to see the world like a little kid. I saw it like that, now I'm seeing it like I'm seeing it now.

She stood up and the blanket fell away from her and she walked backward along the rooftop, her hair blowing a little by the side of her face. I want to see everything new, she said and she turned her back on him and walked farther out on the roof, waving the cigarette out toward the night sky. I want to feel everything like it's the first time I'm doing it.

Come on back and sit down, he called after her.

She flicked away the tail end of the cigarette and

held both her arms out like wings. What if we could fly? she said. What if it was like we were ghosts and could float around at night and look in people's windows and go through walls and watch what everyone else was doing and they couldn't see us?

I think it would get pretty lonely, he said. They couldn't see you, they couldn't touch you. You couldn't make any difference in whatever they did. That would get pretty old after a while.

She was at the very edge of the roof. I don't know, that might not be so bad. You couldn't touch them but they couldn't touch you either. You'd just fly around free.

Beyond her the other rooftops of the neighborhood rose half-visible in the streetlights and then beyond that no rooftops at all, just the lights beaming like little white crosses and then dark beyond that. She teetered a little as she looked out and he stood and started toward her. Besides, he said. I don't think that's how it is with ghosts.

You don't?

He walked to her and wrapped his arms around her waist. No, I think ghosts can go through things and into things and whatever they touch or whatever they're inside of then they become a part of that and they forget about how they were ever separate from everything else.

I never heard anything like that. She turned and

faced him and put her hands on his shoulders. If that's how it is, then what would you be part of if you could be part of anything?

You, for one thing, he said and she closed her eyes and smiled.

He kissed her forehead and said why didn't they go on back in, it was cold outside and they walked back across the roof, Jennifer leaning close to his chest. He picked up the blanket on the way and then helped her through the open window and she walked backward and sat on the bed and he leaned into her, kissing her mouth and touching his fingers to her face.

I guess the Ouija board was right, she said. Tonight is the night. Both of them lay back and he kissed down her neck and shoulder, down her arm and turned it over gently and kissed downward and along the scar on her wrist and a shudder passed all the way through her when he did. He moved up and pulled his shirt off over his head and the room was cold but it didn't matter.

Roy and Donna stopped at two houses that looked like family homes with swing sets in the yard and one with a dog and the other with a station wagon parked in the drive. They went to a high-rise with rings of white lights looped like a necklace all the way down and then to a desolate motel and it was getting close to midnight by the time they stopped at the bar called Veronica's.

What is this place, a strip joint or something? Donna asked, looking at the neon outline of the dancing girl on the roof, and Roy said, What the hell do you care, they sell liquor here.

That was true, she couldn't argue with that, and she sat at the bar while Roy disappeared into the backroom in the company of the tall girl with the red leather boots. There was a stage with a catwalk and red and blue lights, mirrors and shining chrome poles, and there was a tiny girl in half a T-shirt tending bar and the bar itself so polished Donna could see her own reflection, a colored blur, a smashed distortion of herself, and wasn't that perfect, wasn't that just about the way she felt anyway, and what if the Human Services people found out she came to a place like this? What kind of mother would they think she was, sitting here in the spinning lights with all the girls whirling in their pasties and the men's naked faces and pitchers and glasses lined up like an arsenal in the cold part of the night? Wouldn't they just love to write a report about something like this?

But that was something to think about tomorrow, she told her reflection in the bar. There was no help for any of it now. Tomorrow she could figure out what to do and she ordered her drink and two dancers on stools at the end of the bar nodded her way, giggling together over their cigarettes, their bangs almost touching as their heads leaned in. The rum and Coke came and then a man at her side, tall and hollow-cheeked, a faded western shirt and an Adam's apple so big it seemed almost to be staring at her itself. Why don't I buy you your next drink, the man said in a high, country drawl.

She couldn't look into his eyes and studied the frayed place on his shirt where a button was missing. I'm here with somebody, she said, but thanks anyway, and she turned away to her drink, thinking how a place couldn't get any sadder than this with the working girls traipsing around in their underwear and some fifty-year-old country boy with exaggerated ideas about women in the city, but he was still there, leaning on the bar beside her now and he wasn't going to be the type to take no for an answer. He kept pressing and she kept refusing until finally she couldn't take it and tried to move away, nearly falling over the bar stool, her drink spilling to the floor, and Hell, he said, forget you. Who do you think you are anyway?

The colored lights cut across the barmaid's blank face and the dancing girls' shadowed eyes and in their locked stares she saw that same question, Who do you think you are? Everybody around looked as though they could tell she didn't know the answer, and what could she do now but stand there and shatter into pieces, either that or rattle the glass half-spilled back onto the bar and walk away. So that was it. She turned and started through the tables, focusing solely on the front door, taking careful steps as she went, as if each one came completely from a memory of some way she used to walk before.

Outside, the truck was locked and she leaned against the fender, her arms hugged around her and the streetlights like blades of ice. She cursed Roy Dale for thinking so little of her to bring her to a place like this, and what had she ever been thinking anyway, worrying about how he would feel if she broke it off with him? Of course he wouldn't even care and of course Maggie was right about how she took up with him in the first place because he could never really matter. But it was something even more than that too, something worse, for all the good it did to see these things now when whatever the quality was that had made her otherwise before had been broken away. And that's who she was, a broken person doing broken things with a broken man.

She paced in front of the truck and nursed her anger because it was all she had and when he finally came out, she launched at him, and Don't ever do this to me again, she said, almost spitting the words. Don't ever take me with you if you have this shit to do. I don't want any part of it anymore, do you hear me?

He grabbed her wild arms and she struggled but he pinned her to the side of the truck. What the hell's the matter with you now, he said, the look in his eyes like he could kill her dead and never think twice, and

You smoke up my dope all night long and now you're gonna act like I got no business selling it? I got news for you, you don't tell me what to do, and she couldn't hold back the tears and all her fight seeped away. He let go of her and she sank against the truck. Shit, he said, what are you gonna do, go and get all moral on me? It's too late for that coming from you. Hell, your own boy and that wild little girlfriend of his are out selling dope to a bunch of camouflage-wearing crazy bastards and you're gonna give me a hard time, well, you can forget that kinda shit.

She looked up at him, wiping at her eyes with the cuff of her jacket, and What are you talking about? she said. What do you mean about Wesley?

He walked toward the driver's side door and she pulled at his arm. Tell me, she said, What do you mean? He looked away toward the street, his jaw muscles working, and Don't get yourself all bent out of shape, he said. It's just some small time stuff. Him and his girlfriend just making a little extra cash, that's all, nothing big.

She tightened her grip on his arm and there weren't any more tears. It doesn't matter what you think of me, she said, measuring the words slowly. I don't have time to go around worrying about that, I've got my boys to raise and I'm not going to let you drag them into any of this. I told you that before and there better not be any more reason to say it again.

Wesley waited in the parking lot in front of the high school but Jennifer never came. When he got home later that afternoon he asked his mother if there had been any telephone calls for him but she wasn't thinking about anything like that. She called him into the kitchen and told him to sit down at the table across from her. Her face was washed out and her faded blue sweater had lost all its form and hung long and loose, the misshapen cuffs unraveling around her fingers. Her glass sat on the table in front of her and as she started to talk she moved it back and forth cautiously, like a chess piece she couldn't afford to lose. I want to know what you think you're doing, she said without looking up at him. Don't you know they can put you in prison for selling marijuana? Don't you know that? Or do you just not care?

What are you talking about? Wesley said. I'm not selling marijuana, and her lips tightened and she told him there wasn't any use in lying about it. Roy Dale had let it slip and she knew all about how he and his little girlfriend were selling dope like it was nothing but some kind of after-school job and she knew he wasn't that stupid so it must be her, it must be that new girlfriend, and if he couldn't think for himself when he was around her then he better keep away because girls like her never came to any good.

Her lips trembled now, her hand fluttered like a wounded bird up from her glass and into her hair, but she still never raised her eyes. It wasn't fair to talk about Jennifer that way but Wesley only folded his hands in front of him and kept his voice low. You don't know anything about Jennifer, he said. You don't know what she's like. But her anger was rising now and she handled it awkwardly, like something she might lose her grip on any second, and she told him not to tell her what she didn't know. She could see how things were and where they were going and goddammit she was going to head them off before it got any worse and what would his father think?

But that was crossing the line. That was going too far and Wesley stood up from the table, his chair screeching on the floor and tumbling back. Don't tell me what my father would think about me, he said. Don't even bring that up with you seeing Roy Dale and what have you got in that glass, some more liquor already at this time of day?

Wait a minute here, she said, looking up at him now. You just sit back down.

But he didn't sit down and I don't know why I don't just give up on you. Drinking all the time and leaving frozen dinners out for us and Nelson's going around talking about how he wishes he could move in with somebody else. So don't even try acting like you're my mother again all the sudden because it's not gonna work.

She stared at him, the expression on her face like he'd struck her. You don't talk to me that way, she said. Don't, she said, don't, and her voice trailed away and the resolved set of her face collapsed and she bowed her head over the table.

For a moment Wesley stood on the far side of the table watching her and the whole room seemed to fill with aching. I'm sorry, he said finally.

I don't want to lose you, she said, her head still bowed. I don't want to lose you and Nelson, but I don't know what to do. He went to her side and started to put his hand on her shoulder but held back and her shoulders heaved and her trembling fingers picked at the loose threads on her sleeve.

Maybe we oughta go outside and do something, Ragel said and Nelson said, Like what? and Ragel said he didn't know, just something.

Nelson looked at the window and even the glass seemed to shiver against the gray sky. It's too cold out there, he said. I like to froze to death just coming over here, and Ragel said he knew it, it sure was cold. The water was solid in the birdbath out back and the neighbor's garden hose broke off in chunks.

Nelson lay on the floor looking up at the ceiling and Ragel lay with his back in the seat of the recliner, his legs draped over the armrest. The living room bloomed with plants, deep green ones with fronds the size of outstretched hands, and vines falling down from the deep-burnished shelves. A red-and-gold afghan spread across the back of the couch and behind that on the wall a painting of three boats on a riverbank clustered together like a small family, safe from whatever it was down in that river behind them.

On the floor next to Nelson, a peanut butter and jelly sandwich sat on a broad plate and he took up one half and laid the other half on his stomach. You know how the grass gets all hard and yellow in the winter? he said and Ragel said that he did. Nelson took a bite from the sandwich and said, I wonder what happens when it gets to be spring again, does that grass turn back green or does new grass come in over it?

I think the new grass comes in over it, Ragel said.

So what happens to the old grass then?

Well, I guess the old grass just goes on back into the earth and then it gets recycled and all like that.

Nelson thought about that for a while and it seemed to him that such a process would have to take a very long time, but he could see no other way it could be. He could see no room among the dry husks and crumbling branches outside for anything like ghosts or heavens.

Lejeune came down the hall then and stopped at the edge of the room and planted her hands on her hips. You must be the two laziest boys I ever seen in the world, she said. Look at you laying around eating peanut butter and jelly sandwiches like there isn't a care on this earth. She laughed and walked around the corner into the kitchen but the warmth of her lingered in the room.

After a while Nelson's mind wandered in another direction and he pictured Melinda sitting next to him by the roadside. He thought about what they had talked about and finally he asked Ragel had he ever had a girlfriend before, and Ragel said not really, he'd come close to it once but there really wasn't much to it and then she got mad at him and he never did know what for. How come? Ragel said. Do you like somebody or something?

Nelson studied the family of boats on the wall and I don't know, he said. It's just I played football with that friend of your sister's the other day and she's real good. I know she's in high school and all like that but she said I could go out to her dad's farm with her sometime and I was thinking I might do it.

You oughta go, Ragel said. That would probably be a real good time out there. He explained how his grandparents owned a farm down outside of Tyler, Texas, and he visited there about four times a year. It's one of the most fun kind a things there is, he said. They got horses to ride and everything else. We always go on Christmas break and spend a whole week down there.

Nelson rolled over on his side and looked up at Ragel. Are you going down there this Christmas break too? he asked and Ragel said that he was, the whole family was going, and Nelson rolled back and looked out the window at the cold sky, not saying anything.

Maybe I could ask my parents if you could go with us this year, Ragel said after a while. I bet they'd say okay because Lejeune took one of her girlfriends down there with her last summer.

Was it Melinda? Nelson asked.

No, it wasn't Melinda, it was another friend.

Oh, Nelson said and looked at the window again. I don't know if I could ride those horses, he said but Ragel told him it didn't matter. There were always other things they could do, like swinging from a rope down into the hay in the barn or exploring for diamonds in their cave by the river.

Nelson pictured a cave full of diamonds and a big farmhouse with a round barn and a corral filled with horses rearing up and stamping the dust. He pictured Ragel's father hoisting him up onto the back of a sorrel stallion with a silver-studded saddle, a wild look in the horse's eyes and snuffling out through its nostrils, Ragel's father holding the reins, saying, Steady boy, steady, and the horse calming down, the wildness still there, only all under control.

I sure wouldn't mind going down there, he said finally. I wouldn't mind that at all. It wouldn't be an easy thing to ask his mother though, he knew that, but he didn't know why she should care one way or the other. His own home didn't even seem as real anymore as a diamond mine farm and anyway she would probably be with that man, him holding onto her around the waist and the two of them staring at each other like no one else existed at all.

There had been good days in the past, even in the depths of winter, sunshine and the blue sky and the whole family there, but Donna could only feel bits of them now, small and scattered shards that she could see no way to fit back together. It felt like work cut out for somebody else but no one had ever come to do it. So she waited until midnight, when Wesley and Nelson were both in bed, and she lit a candle on the kitchen table and took out the bottle from the cupboard. She was going to make a ceremony out of emptying it into the sink but as she stood just beyond the ring of candlelight she faltered, thinking maybe it would be better to keep it around just for a reminder and that would take more strength anyway, wouldn't it? To have it always there and to never give in?

She stayed up and tried to read an old book of poems in the living room and then finally went to bed but the grotesques returned in that time just before sleep, the tumescent faces and outstretched hands, only with even more substance this time, and she struggled out of the tangled sheets and turned on the light to prove to herself they weren't really there. Nothing was there but her and the empty room and the wall heater ticking to the side of the window.

She left the light on and pulled down the poems again, spread the book open against her legs and forced herself to concentrate on the words. For a long time she read, whether she comprehended or not, the rhythm of the lines giving form to her thinking, and deep into the pages, when the words opened up, she saw the ice drive to the center of the fallen tree and that was right, that was the way it was. On the one side here she was frozen and on the other her life drove through her like a green stem and in the middle Jack lay on the floor with the blood in his hair.

On the first side the future and past infused whatever she did but now that was all a broken trust and every moment she lived was as brittle as the ice that glazed everything it set down on in the winter. One time the future and the past wound around each other and life expanded outward like the branches of a tree. Days of Jack in the swimsuit with the totem-pole heads, making muscle-man arms at the side of the lake, the boys waist deep in green water, herself diving headfirst down from the rocks, plunging through the smooth surface. The past and the present and their whole futures together in those moments but how could she look at the world in that way anymore with this deep scar down the middle? There was no way that she could and the moment had passed for wishing she could make time turn around or stop or swallow her up and she would have to walk out with the knowledge that at any moment life could go wrong, the way an airplane flying through low-hanging clouds could crash into the side of a mountain without any warning, and that knowledge was inside of everything now.

She arose from her bed and walked down the cold hall, past where her boys slept, and stood at the living-room window looking out. The glass shivered in the wind and the sky beyond was dark and starless but the wind and the dark meant no harm, they just went about their business, always dependable in their own unswayable manner, like time and the fact that people came and stayed and then went away.

The next evening she sat studying the yellow pages from Tulsa and she never would have thought there would be such a long list of counselors and centers and schools for the drunk and addicted. So many people going off to such places to give over their hurt to strangers and the strangers prodding and poking into all your secret rooms, all the secret rooms you could hardly go into yourself, the secrets that changed shape and slipped away every time you tried to grab hold. Something about it seemed shameful and weak, but where else could you go anymore? Who could you turn to now in this world with the way it was?

She was reading over the friendliest names but had not yet found one worth underlining when Nelson crept into the kitchen and stopped on the far side of the table, his face serious and his fingers fumbling together in front of him. He started but stopped and looked away and she folded her hands over the open telephone book. What is it? she asked him. Come here and sit down.

He put his hand on the back of the chair but remained standing, and she tried to shut out every other thought except for him. I was wondering, he said staring at the chair, if I could go with Ragel to his grandparents' house for Christmas break this year. He's gonna be gone for a week.

She stared at him, blinking as though she could bring him into focus and find out he meant something else, but he didn't, he only meant he would rather leave for the holiday than spend it with her and for a second she saw how it must have looked through his eyes, days off from school in an empty house and nothing to do but play whatever game it was that he played in the dry field out back.

He started to say something more but she said, Wait a minute now. Hold on right there. Holidays are for the family to spend together. You need to stay home, you need to be here with us. I'll make sure we have a good Christmas here.

But he didn't understand that and went on about horses and a cave by a river and how he'd never been to a farm and when she said that he could go some-time later maybe, he looked up at her, the tears held back in the corners of his eyes. But Ragel's the only friend I really have, he said, and you'll be with Roy Dale anyway.

For a second her hand wavered in front of her, she didn't know what it was doing, it rose by itself and she forced it into her lap. No I won't, she said. I'll be here with you and so will Wesley. We'll have a tree and you can hang the bulbs on it like we used to. But he said he didn't want to hang bulbs and didn't care about a tree and Wesley wouldn't be there either, he'd be with his girlfriend or maybe he'd be out somewhere with Roy Dale again too, the way he was tonight.

Wesley's not with Roy, Donna said. He's at work.

No he's not. He's with that Roy Dale. He told me he was gonna go meet him and they were gonna take a drive somewhere.

Donna looked at the yellow pages, all the words and numbers bleeding together on the page, and she clamped her lips together, folded the book closed and stood up from the table.

What about going down to the farm with Ragel? Nelson asked as she started to turn away, and she stopped. You're staying here for Christmas, she said, and that's all there is to it. You can visit that farm some other time. Now go get your coat. I'm calling Maggie and we're going out. There's something I have to get settled that I should have settled before now.

The night was cold and clear and the cinder-block buildings along the side of the road seemed frozen in place. Roy lit a cigarette and cracked the passenger-side window, leaned against the door and studied Wesley's face, the narrowed eyes and the straight line of his mouth. Something was going on here and Roy didn't know what it was. Maybe it was the girl, maybe Wesley had found out about that, but what could you do, she was a wild thing and would do what she damn well pleased.

Wesley turned east where the road darkened and lowered the volume on the radio and it wasn't about his girlfriend, it was about his mother. She was like someone who had been sick for a long time, he said, and she was weak from it and needed time to get her strength back. He didn't know if Roy knew about his father and what happened to him, but things had never been the same since then and she couldn't seem to get herself back on track, and Roy knew all about that kind of thing. He knew all about your father being gone and who the hell cared. Wesley kept talking and Roy looked at him silently, thinking, That's a sad story but you're lucky your old man got killed when he did, it saved you from all the beatings you'd have to take when you got big enough to hit and getting locked in the cellar and treated like a dog.

Then the point of it came. Wesley knew he couldn't tell Roy what to do but he thought it would be best if he backed off from seeing his mother. Roy just looked at him and nodded, took a drag off his cigarette, then threw the butt out the window. Well hell, isn't that something, he said. You don't even understand what your mother and me got going. She likes it just like it is, pardner, and I don't think she'd appreciate you getting in the middle of things. Who's the parent of who in your family anyway?

Wesley stared ahead and didn't answer and after a long moment Roy said, You know, it's funny but just the other day she had the idea it was you that needed to stay away from me but here you are, and I guess when you want some extra pocket money you'll show up on my doorstep asking if you can't sell a little dope too.

That's the other thing, Wesley said. I'm through with any of that kind of thing and so is Jennifer.

Roy coughed out a short dry laugh and Is that so? he said. Did you ask her about that?

I'm just telling you, Wesley said.

Roy studied his face awhile longer, took a long pull on the beer, then looked out the window. The machine shops and warehouses were only shadows in the darkness separated by empty lots and scrub oaks, and he looked back at Wesley. You better talk to Jennifer, he said. I don't think she's gonna see it that way.

Wesley said that was all right, he knew her better than Roy did and Roy smiled at that. I'll tell you what then, he said. You just ask her if she doesn't want that pound of dope she's supposed to come by for tomorrow. And while you're at it, ask her if she wants me to stop driving her out to that motel to see Colby on Thursdays. You ask her that one too.

A change came into Wesley's eyes then, a barely restrained anger that Roy didn't like the look of. If it came down to a fight then Roy would hurt him if he had to, but Wesley didn't say anything, he only clenched tightly to the steering wheel and stared straight ahead until they reached the little shopping center at the edge of town. Get out, he said, pulling up to the curb. You can call someone to come get you from here, but I don't want to ever have to talk to you one more time again.

Roy looked him over but he never turned. I'm not getting out here, Roy said. How do you expect me to get home?

You've got friends, don't you?

I don't know what you're getting all pissed off for. I was just telling you how it was. If anyone oughta be pissed, it's me.

Wesley didn't say anything then, he only gripped the steering wheel and kept staring through the windshield and Roy said, Shit. All right then. All right, I'll get on out, but you're gonna be seeing me again. You can count on it. He stepped out and as the car pulled away, he watched the taillights growing smaller and he couldn't help thinking that it was more than just his ride home that was trailing off down the road. But he knew it didn't have to be that way. He could have played it just the opposite with the boy, he could have told him his mother was the only worthwhile thing to come along in his life in more time than he could keep track of. He could have said he'd try to be different with her from now on.

The parking lot was mostly empty and half the stores in the shopping center were already closed. The wind whipped across the pavement, scattering plastic and paper, and Roy's worn leather jacket wasn't warm enough for a night like this one.

Maggie said she thought she could find it, but they drove down the gravel roads in the dark, Donna on the passenger side and Nelson in the back, and there was no ranch as Roy had described it couched in the dormant fields or back in the clusters of dead trees. There were only ramshackle wood houses and wasted trailers and the remnants of shacks half-crumbled to the ground. Maybe we should go on back, Maggie said, but Donna said no, she wasn't about to let Roy get Wesley in any more trouble.

Finally they stopped at a small clapboard house right where she thought the ranch should be and she and Maggie went to the door to ask for directions. The yard was cluttered with the dry bones of misshapen scrub oaks and rusted tin trash bins piled to the rims with garbage. The porch sagged inward toward the middle and gave in even more as they stepped up to the door and knocked on the gray chipped frame, a hollow sound that seemed too loud against the dark.

Finally the door opened and a small, wild-haired silhouette stood against the crack of light and an old woman's rusty voice asked what did they want this time of night, even though it was only just after eight. Donna asked about Roy Dale's ranch and the old woman stepped out now, the light catching the side of

her cracked parchment face, and Ranch? she said. Roy
Dale's ranch? Is that what that fool told you? Roy Dale
tell you he had him a ranch? Her face parted into a
thin, sliced smile and then a hoarse laugh and a cloud
of smoke and then coughing and You're as big a fool as
him if you believed that line of bull.

Donna asked her what she meant and the old
woman's eyes narrowed and she looked Donna up and
down. I don't see what someone like you's doing with
that outfit Roy anyway, she said, and Donna said, What
are you talking about, what do you mean? The old
woman told her then, she was Roy's Aunt Boots and
Roy didn't do anything but sleep in a camper shell out
back and paid her twenty-five dollars a month to shower
and eat there and a goddamn ranch, that was a good
one, she'd have to remember that. Roy Dale running
a ranch like he was Gene Autry or somebody. Like he
was Roy Rogers and Trigger.

When they drove away Maggie never said I told
you so and Donna appreciated that. She stared into the
headlight glare and nobody mentioned the leukemia
lies or Arabian horses or the ranch where troubled kids
could come in the summer. None of that mattered
now, it was only Wesley that mattered and if Roy had
him out at Sam Casey's place loading up marijuana, no
lie would be big enough to hold off what she had to
say about that.

The books had to be somewhere stacked in the attic, the old agronomy textbook and the almanacs, the pamphlets the Department of Agriculture put out on seed and crop rows, winter wheat and alfalfa and worm farms. Sam knew he had put them away for that time when he would need to learn something new but tonight he got lost in the pictures of Melinda instead. They were in the box by the attic window and he sat in the shallow pool of light shuffling them slowly like some antique collection of tarot cards that only augured the past—Melinda got up in his old buckskin jacket and Melinda with the cowboy hat and the corncob pipe and galoshes and then her mother too, laughing with her long hair down on her shoulders.

Outside the window a bright movement caught his eye and the headlights came bouncing around the curve in the road. At first he thought it might be someone bringing Roy back to collect his truck but the car didn't belong to anyone he knew. It stopped beside the truck and two women stepped out and he saw that it was her as soon as she walked out of the dark.

Her hand was just moving up to knock again as he opened the door and she seemed startled to see him, the picture of her so clear cut before him it seemed frozen for a moment, like one of the snapshots from the box in the attic. I'm looking for my son, she said. Wesley. I'm here to take him home, and she moved her head so that her long hair swung out to the side and something like a dare crossed her face, like just you try to tell me I can't.

I haven't seen him, Sam told her. It's been almost a week and the quail are all sold so there's not any reason for him to come by anymore.

Don't give me that, she said. I know you've had him out selling your dope. I know what you've got going on out here.

Sam stepped all the way out on the porch now and set his eyes to hers. He wanted to put his hand on her shoulder and promise he never did any such thing, but he could only say, I don't know what you mean, even though he did. He knew what she meant because he knew Roy Dale.

Well, just let me talk to Roy then, she said. Tell him I want to talk to him right now.

But Roy wasn't there either and when she asked why his truck was parked out in the front, Sam said he must have come by and then gone off with somebody else. Maybe it was with Wesley but he didn't know that for sure and he'd help her if he could, he wanted to help her, but he was telling the truth and if she wanted to wait until Roy got back she was welcome to stay.

Her face softened a little then but the hard edge remained in her eyes. She crossed her arms and nodded toward the car. I have my other boy in the backseat over there, she said. I can't be hanging around here half the night.

You could have him come on inside, Sam said, looking out at the little silhouette in the back of the car. You all could come in and we could talk for a while and I bet Roy'll be back anytime.

I don't know. She shifted from foot to foot and looked back at the car, and before she could decide the telephone rang in the kitchen.

At first Sam thought, Just let it ring, but then it hit him that it might be Roy and he turned out to be right. It was Roy Dale calling from a pay phone and mad about something. He didn't want to talk to Donna, but Sam said he had to. She's all worried sick, Sam told him. And I don't blame her one bit.

Her friend stayed in the car with the boy and she bustled inside, eyes wary and nervous hands at her hair, and waiting in the living room Sam could just barely hear her in the kitchen when her voice raised. Roy wasn't supposed to have anything to do with Wesley, she said, and then something about how they had two different views on the world, she and Roy did, and she didn't see how the two could be reconciled. At first there was a trembling quality to her voice but it firmed as she talked, like a voice tuning in on a radio. She was finding out about Roy now, how he really was, and it was bound to happen sooner or later, the only surprise was that it had taken this long.

He wants to talk to you, she said when she came back from the kitchen, and Sam asked if everything was all right. She looked at him and said yes, every-thing was all right. Then she smiled a small, private smile and said, I guess I should of known I could trust Wesley all along.

He's a good boy, Sam said. He always did a good job with the quail.

Her smile slipped away and she said, No offense, but I still don't want him coming out here anymore or having anything to do with this place.

I'm telling you the truth, he told her. I've never had Wesley doing anything out here but working with the quail. Besides I'm getting out of all that other stuff myself.

Just the same, she said. He's not coming out here anymore. She fixed her eyes on his to punctuate her point and he only nodded in return. She turned then and walked out the door and Sam watched the car drive away for a moment before he went back to the phone. Roy was still upset. He was stranded on the edge of town, he said, the damn kid had left him out there without a ride. Sam paused for a second and looked around his empty kitchen. If things had been different she might still be there sitting at the table but things were like they were, and Okay, he said finally. Just hold on, Roy. I'll come out as soon as I can.

Nelson asked Wesley what if he called that Melinda girl to see whether she might want to go out to her father's farm like she talked about doing and Wesley told him he had something else he had to do this morning. He would have to take care of that first but he might be talking to Melinda later on and he'd see what she had to say then. You'll just have to wait, he said and Nelson didn't say anything back, he only turned and walked to his room. He put on his coat and his gloves and the green cap, which would have to do, because he didn't have a plastic army helmet like Ragel had.

The field behind the house was frozen and the yellow grass hung over sideways as if it were trying to curl up and get warm. Nelson broke off a twig from one of the small trees, stripped it clean of its crackled brown leaves and held it up to take aim. The enemy is out there, he said. All around. And it's our mission to track them down and eliminate them before they can take everything over. That's what they want to do, take over all the houses and the school and everything else.

Ragel wasn't there, he was already gone to his grandparents' farm, so Nelson could only pretend what he would say. Is it aliens from another planet out there? he imagined Ragel asking, and he answered back, No, this time they're from here.

The wind blew cold across the field and stung his face as he walked forward with the stick cradled and ready to fire. All the trees across the creek stood bare and the sky was gray. At the low, sloping bank he stopped and the ice on the water looked barely thick enough to walk on but there was nothing else to do but go forward. I'll try it first, he told Ragel, and here I'll tie a rope around my waist and you hold onto the other end in case I go down.

Underneath his feet he felt the water moving but he kept on, his hands held out to his sides like a tight-rope walker's hands, until he set foot down on the other side. Now you come across too, Ragel, he said, and this time I'll hold onto the rope for you.

He waited there in the grass then, his hands outstretched, the ice creaking, nearly cracking under the weight, the threat of enemy fire all around, but still he held fast to the rope until finally Ragel stood beside him and he had only just stepped onto the bank when the mortar shell burst into the water right where they

227

both had crossed, blasting Nelson back into the thick curls of yellow grass, and I'm hit, he called out. I'm hit.

Ragel was right there beside him then, leaning down. Where did they get you, buddy? Is it bad?

A piece of shrapnel, Nelson said weakly, lying on his back looking up at the gray sky. I got caught in the head, buddy. Right over my eye.

I see it, Ragel said, touching his fingers next to the wound. You're bleeding pretty bad. Do you think you can keep going?

Nelson paused for a long moment, looking at the sky, the blood running down his forehead and along the side of his face. Yeah, he said finally. I've gotta keep going. I'm not gonna let you face them all by yourself.

Ragel helped him up then and they started up the far bank heading straight into the sights of the enemy and Nelson with the blood in his eyes so that the whole world looked red, but he never said anything about that, he just kept moving ahead with Ragel at his side.

Her mother said wait and was gone a long time and Wesley waited until the telephone was hot against his ear. Finally she returned and told him that no, Jennifer wasn't home and there was no telling where she'd gone off to already this morning. He gave her his name and she acted as though she'd never heard it before, repeating it twice like some foreign word she couldn't understand. When she hung up he sat transfixed, picturing the inside of the steakhouse and Colby across the table with his smirks and sly-eyed glances in the secondhand light.

Melinda was home though and he told her he would be right over. She said all right and there was a seriousness in her voice, as though she already knew what it was all about. Her half sister's little metal swingset stood near the chain-link fence in the backyard and they sat side by side in the swings, both looking at the ground, arms wrapped around the chains and hands in their coat pockets, and a feeling of last things that was all too familiar. He finally started. It's about Jennifer, he said and she said that she thought that it probably was.

He told how he had called her for the last two days and she never was there and never called back, but he didn't want to say anything now about what Roy Dale had told him. He didn't want to put any truth into it. I was just wondering if she'd talked to you, he said. I thought maybe she was mad at me about something.

She rocked back and forth slightly in the swing, her shoes dragging in the leaves, and her voice was somber when she spoke. I've known Jennifer longer than anyone almost, she said. She was my first friend when I moved into town here with my mother.

She paused and looked away at the house. But

sometimes she does things that I guess are kind of self-ish and that's just how she is.

Wesley watched her face closely, thinking of how Jennifer had said nearly the same thing about her, but he couldn't see it in Melinda's face or the way she held herself. I don't know, he told her, but I always thought Jennifer might of got hurt somehow and she's just try-ing to make up for it with the way she acts now.

Melinda nodded. It was her parents, she said, her father always gone doing something about oil and her mother in one club after another and neither of them really mean or violent but they never had time for their own daughter.

But it seems like it must be something more than just that, Wesley said. I mean, I've seen the scar on her wrist and she's never talked about it but it seems like something pretty bad must of happened for her to go and do that.

I don't know, Melinda said. I sure wouldn't want to live that way, like you weren't anything but a ghost wandering the halls at your own house.

I guess, Wesley said, but that's a slow kind of thing, not something that hits you all at once.

Melinda sat quiet for a long moment, twisting the thin leather watchband on her wrist. There was an-other thing too, she said finally. Two summers ago Jennifer's uncle had come to stay while her father was gone on business and the uncle was from California and looked like you'd think a surfer would look and then it was later in August after he left, Jennifer pulled away from everybody and then all of a sudden she was gone and Melinda only found out later they put her up in St. Francis in the psychiatric wing. When she finally came back she showed off the scars and all she would say was if you knew what was good for you just forget about love.

So what are you saying? Wesley asked. You think something happened with her uncle?

You'll have to ask her about that, Melinda said. I don't want to start saying things Jennifer wouldn't want me talking about. You know, it's like I said, she's the oldest friend I have and my father always told me you have your regular family and then you have the one you find along the way and that's how it is with Jennifer and me. She might not always act like I think she should, and I'll let her know it too, but I'm still going to try to be the same kind of friend I'd want for myself.

Wesley looked down at the ground for a while and then back up. But I guess it isn't too good, he said. I mean, it isn't looking too good with her and me, and Melinda said that was one of those things he would have to ask Jennifer about.

They both sat swinging gently in the cold and neither one spoke for a long moment. Small snowflakes were coming now, spiraling around them and disappearing into whatever they touched.

You know, my brother has a big crush on you, he said finally. He's all the time asking me when you're going to take him out to your dad's farm. A friend of his went off to visit at his grandparents' farm for Christmas and now he's got it all set in his head that he has to go out to one too. He says you and him talked about it that time we went out to Jennifer's cousin's place, but I just tell him you're probably too busy.

She looked over and smiled. I'm not too busy. I was probably going out there sometime this weekend anyway. Just let me know when a good time would be and we'll fix it up.

Really? It wouldn't be too much trouble?

It wouldn't be any trouble at all.

Nelson will sure be glad to hear it.

You know what? she said. I wouldn't be too surprised if Jennifer didn't get back home around three o'clock or so.

Three o'clock?

Uh-huh. Her eyes narrowed. You know, the thing with Jennifer is sometimes it's best if you don't let her have her own way.

He stood up from the swing. Thanks, I'll try to keep that in mind. But she's got a way of making you forget things like that, if you know what I mean.

Melinda looked up at him. Yeah, I guess I do.

It was just after three when Wesley pulled up in front of the white house. Jennifer said come in, they could talk in the kitchen, never mind her parents, they never paid any attention to anything anyway, but he said no, why didn't they talk outside. They sat in the car and he started the engine and turned on the heater and the light snow fell down around the windows. I love snow, she said. I wish it snowed in the summer so I could take off all my clothes and run in it naked.

I told Roy Dale we weren't going to be having anything to do with him anymore, Wesley said, staring straight toward the windshield, and she asked him how come. She said she knew Roy was a strange character but where else were they going to get such a good batch of dope. Still staring ahead Wesley said, I told him we didn't need anything more from him and he said I better ask you about that. He said I better ask you about whether you wanted him to keep driving you up to see that lawyer in Tulsa.

Oh, she said and that was all she said for a second and it was all she needed to say. The engine coughed then hummed in time to the sound of the heater. Well, you can't believe what all Roy Dale tells you, she added on finally but it didn't matter now. The world couldn't have seemed any more changed if the snow had turned to black and the sky to a bleeding red.

I don't know what I was thinking, he said, I guess I was making you up, like a kid trying to pretend things aren't like they are, dreaming up flying space-ships and planets where nothing ever dies.

Anyway we never said we weren't going to see anyone else, she said and he looked at her now. She was turned and her hair hung down along the side of her face, almost hiding the small line of her mouth, and she sniffed but only from the cold and not from crying.

No, he said. We never said that.

So I don't know what you have to be mad about, she said looking down, picking at a thread on her jeans, and he told her he wasn't mad, it was more like the feeling when somebody dies.

Well, maybe that's the way you'd like it then, if I was just dead and then you wouldn't have to mess with me anymore at all.

You know that's not what I mean, he said evenly. I don't even mean I don't ever want to see you any-more and if you need something or someone to talk to you can call me, don't think that you can't do that, but the one thing I'm not gonna help anyone do anymore is kill themselves, I won't help you with that and what-ever it is you need to get over, you're gonna have to get over it yourself because nobody else can do that kind of thing for you.

Well, that's all right, she said. I don't need you to help me with anything, you didn't really turn out to be how I thought you would be anyway, and he told her he guessed that was probably all for the best.

She looked at him then and said she didn't know what else to tell him and he said that was okay because there wasn't anything left to say. She sat there staring straight ahead for a moment, as though waiting for him to take it all back but he didn't and finally she opened the door. When she walked away she walked part of the way backward, staring into the car, a question left on her face, like maybe she had just started to think about what he was trying to tell her, and then she turned into the falling snow and he drove down the street before she could disappear altogether.

The next day, when Melinda stepped into the car, she smiled at Wesley, the kind of pained smile that told him she knew what had happened between Jennifer and him. But that was all, she didn't say anything about it. Instead she turned to Nelson and asked if he was ready to have some fun. He said that he was and she told him that was good because she was too.

You can count me in on that, Wesley said.

As they drove up the winding road to the farm, the snowflakes meandered down as big as pennies in the air. During the night a light powder had collected and now a thicker layer began to soften the hard fields and the bare branches of the trees. If it comes any faster, Nelson said, we'll have us enough to sled on before we have to go back. If we just had a sled. And Melinda turned in the front seat and told him when she was little her father used to let her sled on a baking pan down the gullies out in the woods.

Wesley parked beneath the tree and when they got out he watched Nelson walk next to Melinda as they started toward the barn and he'd never thought about having a sister before. Do you know my friend James up at school? he asked and she said that she did.

He's a good guy, he said.

I know it, she said, walking on. He's real nice.

At the front of the barn, she told about the games she had played inside of it when she was a girl but they didn't go in and instead circled around back and looked off at the trees where she had been a cavalry scout through most of first grade. Nelson wanted to know if they ever had horses and she said no but they'd once had a tractor and a Labrador retriever named Gordon that was almost big enough to ride on himself. They had a tire swing in the tree out front and people over all the time and music on the front porch, back a long time ago when she was only little and her mother and father were still together.

The snow landed on their sleeves and in their hair and melted and then came again as they walked. Nelson turned in a slow circle in front of them and looked up at the sky and Melinda said it used to be the Sunshine People. That was what they called them-selves back even before she was born. The way it was they tried to start their own little country, all of them together back in the woods. They rented the land and fixed up the house and some of them lived in tents and there was a geodesic dome down to the south by the pond. Her father said it worked for a while and they raised things and made cracked wheat bread and pottery and fixed motorcycle engines. Babies were born right there in the house. They had their own constitution and all it said was We.

And so what happened? Wesley asked her and she said it fell apart. Some of them quit working and just lived off the others. Some of them said just look at the lilies of the field and the others said, Well that's all fine but don't take advantage then when we toil and spin. There were fights and a boy from Malaysia died from the flu. They found him on the floor with his shoes off and a bottle of gin leaked out on the rug. People moved away and others came in looking for a handout. After a while her father got a job working construction sixteen hours a day. He worked sixteen hours a day for five years and then came back and bought the place for himself and then it was only his friends around and the rest scattered like dandelion feathers into the wind, and her father said the Sunshine People was a country that didn't exist anymore, like Atlantis or America before the Mayflower came.

They circled around the farmhouse and ended up on the porch and Nelson asked did they have a fireplace inside and Melinda said that they did. She said,

Come on in and I'll show it to you but we can't start up a fire until my father gets home, and Wesley said they couldn't wait until then. They had to get going and pick his mom up at work.

Nelson looked toward the front door, disappointed but silent, and Melinda put her hand on his shoulder. Why don't you run in and get her, she told Wesley. We'll stay and look around here some more.

Wesley didn't know about that but he saw the spark in his brother's eyes. You sure it won't be any trouble?

No trouble at all. We'll have us a good time. She stood very straight on the porch and Nelson stood beside her, almost touching her, smiling seriously, like they were waiting to have their picture taken together.

Maggie said she didn't know if it was such a good idea to have Roy coming up to see Donna at work. He seemed like the type who could go off the deep end to her.

I know he does, Donna said. That's why I'd rather meet him up here with people around.

She finished pouring her coffee and told Maggie not to worry, her discussion with Roy was going to be short and to the point and besides it wasn't like they were engaged or anything like that. In the break room, she sat at the little round table among the towers of cardboard boxes and looked down into her coffee cup, rehearsing to herself the things she had to say. There would be no reason to mention what Wesley had told her the night before, though that seemed like the worst thing yet. She could almost forgive Roy for the lying he'd done to her but she couldn't forgive the way he'd helped Jennifer hurt Wesley. But she wouldn't say anything about that because Wesley wouldn't want her too. That was just the way he was and she was thinking about that when the door to the break room opened.

Well, Roy said as he walked in, so you finally decided to stop avoiding me, huh?

Here, why don't you sit down, she told him, motioning to the chair on the other side of the table.

That's okay. I feel like standing.

She said if that was the way he felt she would stand up too. Besides, what I have to say isn't going to take very long. I think you probably know what I've got on my mind anyway.

I don't know, he said, stepping closer as she stood. Are you thinking something like how if you just get rid of old Roy then there's gonna be a stampede of men banging on your door with wedding rings in their pockets? Is that what you're thinking?

She looked down at the floor. No, that's the last thing on my mind.

Or maybe it's just Sam Casey you're thinking about. Well, you can forget about that. There isn't any reason for you to go traipsing back off to his place again because, I'll tell you what, he's a loner and he doesn't have any use for you hanging around out there.

It's not Sam Casey.

Matter of fact, you're lucky I ever took you on myself. Roy stepped closer and she stood firm, clenching her fists at her sides.

Why don't you just take a step back, she said. I'm doing what I have to do for my boys and that's the only explanation I owe you.

He smiled sourly. Look at you. Who do you think you are all the sudden, Steve McQueen, ready to fight me and be the big hero? Shit, what'd I ever do to you?

Nothing. Her hands relaxed and she picked up her coffee cup. You haven't done anything. I've done it all to myself but that's over now.

And you're gonna change your life, is that it? You're gonna be born again. Hell, you can't even get through a week without crawling off up in that bottle of rum, how are you gonna change your life?

I'm just gonna go on with what I have to do, she said, staring him in the eye. And it wouldn't hurt you to take a good look at yourself and all your stories about your big ranch and Arabian horses that don't exist anywhere except in your head.

His face burned red then. Who have you been talking to? Did Sam Casey tell you that? Sam hasn't got any business talking to you about what I do.

Sam Casey didn't tell me anything.

What the hell were you two doing over there the other night then when I called. Why don't you tell me that?

Before she could answer, Maggie swung open the door. Everything okay in here? I could hear you way out there on the shoe rack aisle. She moved next to Donna and grabbed hold of her wrist. I don't think you really need to be here anyway, she told Roy. Why don't you just go on.

He stared at her for a moment and then at Donna, the look on his face like he was trying to decide which one to hit first, but instead he said, Fuck it. Just fuck the both of you. I don't know why I'm wasting my time around here anyway. There's plenty of cashiers with big asses in this world, I don't need you and all your shit about your boys. Just don't come looking for me the next time you get horny because that position's gonna be filled. He walked to the door, stopped and looked back but didn't say anything else before slapping the door open with the flat of his hand.

For a moment the feeling of his anger hung in the room like a contrail slowly breaking apart and then Maggie turned to Donna. You doing all right?

Donna laughed nervously. Yeah, she said. I think so.

The windshield wiper on one side was worn and screeched against the glass, leaving streaks of white where the snow fell and Roy said, Goddamn. He pictured Sam and Donna sitting on the sofa the other night all cozy in the living room and Sam saying, You know that Roy Dale's a liar, he doesn't have any ranch and we aren't partners either, he just works for me when I let him. Why didn't you tell her about the deal I could of made, he thought. Why didn't you tell her how they said Roy we'll give you probation and all you have to do is tell us who you're selling this stuff for, you tell her who went to jail for who, and shit well those days are over now, boss, those days are over for good.

He stopped at the Git-N-Go and bought two six-packs for good measure and back on the whitening road he talked out loud to the glass and cold metal walls and it was all about Sam sitting on Ansel's money and who knew how much more, hidden in the walls or the furniture or buried in the ground like goddamn Long John Silver because everybody knew Sam never spent a dime on himself. And it was time for a little talk about that and maybe for more than just talk if Sam tried any more of his lines about how to treat people right.

The snow on the roof of the farmhouse and the barn and on the limbs of the tree out front gave the whole place an old-fashioned look, like some corny postcard, Roy thought, like a Christmas picture of the all-American home, dad and the kids, a fire on the hearth and all that bullshit that never existed outside of fairy tales. Sam's truck was gone but that was all right, Roy didn't mind waiting, and there was a light on in the kitchen anyway. He would just make himself comfortable and whatever there was worth having Sam could just take it off everything he already owed.

When Wesley saw his mother leaned over in her blue smock in the back of the store everything rose up inside of him at the same time, enough to bring him to tears if he let it. She had been the one left behind and she was the one still trying. It would be hard to stop doing some of the things for her he had been doing but he could see now that sometimes the best way to help was to hold back from doing too much.

Maggie tapped her on the shoulder and when she turned around an awkward expression crossed her face and he walked over and lifted the box of calendars into the shopping cart for her and she told him thanks. Are you just about ready to go? he asked her and he asked it as gently as he could. She put up her smock and picked out a few things for dinner, pork chops and potato boats and chocolate cream pie, the kinds of things she might choose for some special occasion.

The snow flew at a slanted angle and the wind whistled down the side windows as they started toward home. It stuck to the parked cars in the lots along the road and then to the lawns and blasted shrubs in the residential addition, all a white frame around her as she looked through the glass, and she said it was all over with her and Roy Dale. It was a mistake from the outset and she took the blame but things were going to be different now. For a while she was quiet and he stared over the steering wheel and waited. And the house wasn't always going to be cluttered with dirty plates, she said finally, and no more clothes lying around on the floor and no more frozen dinners at night unless she had to work late, and she knew she could have been a better mother and she was sorry for that. He started to tell her it wasn't true but she told him shhh, that she knew it was and he knew it too.

You all have been better boys than I ever could of asked for, she said. But I'm going to need you to help me even more now. I'm going to need you to trust me on some things and I know you feel like you have to make some extra money and you might like Sam Casey, I know he seems like somebody decent, but what he's doing out there is illegal and I don't want you to even go around there anymore. You understand that? That's got to be off limits.

Wesley nodded. There was something different in her voice, something just beginning, and this wasn't the time to mention anything about Nelson and Melinda or the way Sam Casey's farm looked in the winter.

The walls were warm yellow and the counters were green. Nelson asked did they ever have pancakes for dinner and Melinda said sure, in fact if he wanted they could have them together when her father got back, and the door flew open and banged on the wall and Roy Dale stood there in the freezing wind.

Well, I didn't expect to have so much company, he said and swung the door back and kicked it shut as he stepped into the room. He slapped the snow off the sleeves of his leather jacket, and Here you are, little Osgood and Melissa, and Melinda said no, it was Melinda and Nelson, and he put on an expression of regret and said, Oh I beg your pardon, ma'am. I'll make sure and write that down.

He had a brown bottle of beer and stopped to take a drink and then walked across to Melinda and stood beside her next to the sink, leaning in toward her in a way that wasn't right, and the room seemed to draw up into a cramped little box. The bill of his cap shaded the top half of his face and the hard lines cracked down the side of his cheek as he smiled and there was a lilt in his raw voice that shouldn't have been there either. Nelson looked at the window and the door but he couldn't leave now and leave her alone with him.

Roy stared at Melinda's downcast face and talked about the snow and then about how warm the kitchen was and everything so homey. What are you all doing, he said, playing house in here by yourselves while the big boss man's away? And she said she expected him back any second now. In fact he should've been here already.

I'll bet, he said, I'll bet, and the way his mouth worked up at the corner and his eyes narrowed down wasn't any way to look at her for a man of his age and Nelson stood up from the table.

Roy looked at him and said, Little old Nelson's kind of young for you to be playing house with, don't you think? Don't you think you need someone bigger? Someone that can take care of you more? I mean, it's a hard old world out there. You never know what can happen. Mean-ass bastards creeping all around and the next thing you know they show up on your front porch and tear your world clean to hell, isn't that right, Nelson? Isn't that just about the way it happens?

Nelson didn't say anything but still stood his ground and Roy said, No it doesn't do any good to play at being a family. You might as well believe in fairy tales or Jesus. And believe me I know what I'm talking about.

I think I heard a truck outside, Melinda said and Nelson heard it too, the engine rattling then dying and the sound of a door. That must be him, she said.

I remember you when you were just a little old thing yourself, Roy told her, never showing any sign of listening to her at all. I remember you couldn't even get into that tire swing out front by yourself and look at you now. He reached out and pushed her hair back from her neck and stepped in close to her. She pulled away and he laughed.

I'm not kidding, she said. I heard him drive up.

Let him come, he said. It don't make a shit to me. He took another drink, and Nelson said, I heard it too, but Roy didn't pay any attention. You oughta be a little more friendly, he said to Melinda, his face leaning close down to hers. You got good-looking hair, so soft like it is. It's just natural for someone to want to touch it, and he stepped in again and took a strand between his forefinger and thumb and said, Yeah, you got pretty hair, a strange kind of color, and I bet you got a pretty little pussy too. I bet the boys would crawl across hot molten lava just to take a look at that little blond pussy.

She winced and Nelson started toward her but there was a footfall behind him and the shadow fell across the floor as Sam Casey came in from the hall. That's all of that shit, he said.

Roy turned and Well, looky here, he said, if it isn't the big boss man himself, in person.

I want you out of here right now, Sam told him but Roy only smiled and said, Hold on just a second now, there's a little business we have to get straight first.

Your business here is done, Sam said and he took three long steps and grabbed Roy by the jacket. Go on now, get your sorry ass out, he said and slung Roy away toward the door. The beer bottle fell and burst on the floor and Now look what you made me do, Roy said. He straightened up and smoothed out the front of his jacket. Look at this mess. A perfectly good bottle of beer.

Sam stood square in front of him and told him he'd crossed the line this time. I'm telling you to leave, he said, and that's all I'm going to say.

Nelson backed up next to Melinda and she told her father, That's all right, that's all right, he's just being a fool, but Roy wouldn't let it stay. Well now, he said, looking down at the broken shards of glass. Let's see who's crossed whose line here, boss. You wreck everything I got going with my woman, I expect to get a little something in return here.

Sam stepped up and Nelson could just see Roy around his hip. I don't want you ever to come back here, Sam said and Roy tilted his face up so that the bill of his cap cut a black slash down past his eyes and he said That's okay, boss, I can live with that but you're gonna to have to pay me what you owe me first.

You send Charlie out tomorrow and I'll settle up with him but I don't want you back around here at all.

I'm not talking about that piddly little bit you got in mind, Roy said. I'm talking about what you owe me in full for everything I put up with you, Ansel's share included.

If you're talking about that jail time again I don't

owe you anything for that. You never did it for anyone but yourself anyway. The way it looks to me you never did it for any reason but to hang it over my head for the rest of my life.

Is that what you think? Roy said. He walked forward toward Sam and stood just in front of him. Is that what you think? Well, fuck you and your high-minded self-righteous ass, Mr. Bossman. Because you can pay me in cash right now or maybe you'd rather pay me off with this little piece of chicken here, but I'm going to get mine, and his fists clenched at his sides and his jaw thrust up but none of that mattered, Sam's hands were so fast Nelson jumped back, and the big fists dug into the leather jacket. Roy's feet lifted off from the floor and then his whole body swung loose in the air and backfirst into the counter. Sam bent over where he'd collapsed and backhanded him once and swung back again but stopped half the way down. A line of blood marked Roy's lip but his eyes were nothing but hard and black, challenging Sam to swing down again, and it was the first time Nelson had seen a man want to be hit.

But Sam never hit him again. His shoulders sagged and he said, Goddammit Roy, just get out, just go on and get out of here, and he straightened up slowly and turned. You kids go on in the other room, he said and it was plain that there were years of weariness inside of his voice. Melinda put her hand on Nelson's shoulder and they went into the hall and behind them the mumbling voices rising and falling for too long but finally Roy shouted loud enough to be heard, I wouldn't even go to sleep if I was you. I'd look behind me every step I took. Then the sound of the door and Nelson looked up and she didn't say anything but only nodded her head to say it was over.

Aunt Boots was half-drunk on the couch when Roy got there, sprawled out among her corn chips and tamales, and Charlie was in the kitchen trying to make chili but it was stuck to the pan. Forget about that, Roy told him, you can heat it up again later, we've got something to do.

Charlie parted from it sadly and pulled on his coat, and Roy said, I told you we couldn't trust Sam. I told you that bastard would put it to us sometime.

Do you think I'll need a hat and maybe some gloves? Charlie asked, and Fuck your hat and gloves, Roy told him. Just button up your coat and come on, and he explained the rest of it in the truck, how he knew all along Sam would try to cheat them and now he knew it for sure. Their cut of the profits was almost all gone and now Sam was saying he wouldn't hire them for the next year either.

Charlie shook his head and said that didn't sound like Sam, but Roy told him he didn't understand, he trusted people too much. No, Sam wouldn't cheat Ansel or Beeline or Jody, it was different with them, but I'm telling you Charlie, Sam don't respect me and you. He treats us like trash and low character types. He thinks that we're stupid and he can run over us any way that he wants.

Did he say that? Charlie asked, the dull hurt in his eyes. Did he say I was stupid?

Do you know how much money Sam must have out there? He's got to have several hundred thousand stashed back somewhere. He's got a goddamn fortune, that's for sure, and I'll tell you this, we deserve it more than he does.

I don't see how Sam could turn mean like that, Charlie said, and Roy turned to him and Well just look at this, the sonofabitch split my lip wide open and it had just got all healed up from before. He punched me right in the mouth and I'm not about to take that kind of shit, not after all I did for him.

Charlie leaned in and focused closely on the cut and the thin veil of anger crossed into his eyes. That's some fried-out shit, he said. That's some kind of fried-out shit like that, man.

Well, you just remember that when we get there, Roy said, and the truck bucked and rattled on the gravel road, the windshield wiper screeching on the glass and Crimson and Clover on the radio. All around the snow fell harder and blotted out almost everything but the bare fingers of the scrub oaks. The bare fingers of the scrub oaks and up ahead the rust-stained walls of the defunct oil tanks and then the black iron sides of the abandoned pump jacks, their heavy heads bowed to the ground, like the frozen remnants of some extinct breed of animal cut off from their rightful tribe.

When they got home Wesley carried the groceries and his mother unlocked the front door, pausing a second to reach up and straighten the loose metal numbers so that the address read the way it should. Wesley tried to make an excuse to leave without mentioning Nelson or anything about Sam Casey but she said she would need help in the kitchen. She thought Nelson would be here by now, she said, but he must be at Ragel's. And that was okay, they'd drive over right now and bring him straight home.

Wesley told her he'd go by himself, he even started toward the door, but that wasn't good enough for tonight and he could see it was all set in her mind how it would be, they'd all be together and this time maybe she meant it.

Just let me get my coat back on, she told him, and you call and tell him we're coming.

Wesley stopped in the doorway between the kitchen and the living room. He's not over at Ragel's, he said, and she stopped and looked up. He's at Sam Casey's. But it's all right, he's with Melinda and he just wanted to look at the farm.

She didn't get angry and her voice didn't rise. She only put on her coat and said, Give me the keys, and she didn't care if her license was suspended or if it would be better for Wesley to drive in the snow, she only said, Give me the keys, and he saw that she meant it and handed the keys to her. She fumbled them at first and then dropped them, but she knelt quickly and picked them up and when she stood, she straightened her back and raised her chin the way she used to do when he was a boy and never questioned whether she meant what she said at all.

Nelson stood at Melinda's elbow as she stirred up the pancake batter and Sam sat cocked back at the table. Flour and eggs and a carton of milk lined the counter and the white powder spotted the cuff of her sweater and she looked down at him and smiled. Sam said maybe he should try calling his mother again to make sure it was all right for him to be out here eating pancakes with dinnertime only a couple of hours away. He didn't want Nelson to get into trouble and he didn't want to get into trouble with her himself, he said, laughing. There was something about the way he sat in his chair at the table, he made the whole room seem like a part of him.

She still wasn't home though and Nelson was relieved that she wasn't. Melinda poured white circles of batter into the big iron skillet and Sam asked didn't

Nelson's mother ever make him pancakes around the house and he said not anymore. They ate frozen dinners mostly nowadays, he said, with the way she worked so much and all like that.

Well, I guess she's got a lot she has to get done, Sam said and Nelson said she sure did.

This is the first time Nelson's been out on a farm, Melinda said. I gave him the grand tour.

It's not much of a farm right now, Sam said. But it's going to be more of one. I've got some ideas about expanding out with the quail and maybe doing something with worms.

Worms? Nelson asked.

Sure, that's a pretty good business to get into. Sell them off for bait to bait shops and that kind of thing. Big old earthworms.

Me and my best friend Ragel always just use the plastic worms and those little lures that look like minnows when we go fishing, Nelson said. I used real minnows once but I didn't like how you had to put the hook through them.

I don't like that either, Sam said. To tell you the truth, anymore when I go fishing I don't care all that much whether I catch anything or not. I just like to go sit out there and enjoy the peace and quiet of it.

That's the same way I am, Nelson said. Me and Ragel, we'll just sit out there and talk. He's down in Texas right now, but he'll be back.

Well, I'll tell you what, Sam said. We have a little pond back in the woods a ways, we'll have to go out there and fish when it gets warm, you and me. How about that?

Nelson said that sounded good and he bet Ragel would like to come too if that would be all right and Sam said sure it would. You couldn't go fishing without your best friend along. That was practically one of the rules of it.

Outside there was the sound of a motor and then a door slamming. Sam sat up and then stood and the mood in the room changed. You all stay in here, he said. His voice was serious and he looked them both in the eye to see that they understood him.

Melinda stopped what she was doing and looked toward the doorway and Nelson stood close to her and looked that way too. There was the sound of Sam at the door and then he said, What are you doing back over here? I told you I didn't want you coming back around, and then Roy Dale's voice answered but Nelson couldn't make out what it was that he said.

Melinda walked into the hallway and Nelson came behind her and they both looked around the door frame to see what would happen.

At first only a sliver of Roy Dale was visible through the screen and then a crack like a pistol shot but it was only Roy's hand on the door as he burst his way through. He barreled straight in without hesitation but Sam stepped aside and Roy nearly fell, his boots sliding beneath him on the hardwood floor. When he'd half-regained his balance, he turned and swung his fist up but Sam dodged away, then grabbed him, wrapping his forearm around his neck, and Roy's feet lifted up, he kicked in the air, his arms swinging wildly, half-choked curses spitting out from his mouth, but Sam hoisted him tighter and Roy's face went red and his hat fell down to the floor.

Then Charlie was there, his small eyes narrowed to slashes, his hands fumbling toward Sam's arm, and You're holding him too tight, he said, you're hurting him, let him go, let him go, but Sam didn't release him. You stay back, Charlie, he said. I'll let him go when he's ready to calm down. You hear me, Charlie, you stay on back over there.

Roy tried to sputter some order and Charlie circled to the side, saying, Come on now, Sam, now you let him go. You let him go or I'm gonna have to make you let him go, and Sam told him he didn't want to do something like that. He said, Charlie, think for yourself just this one goddamn time.

There was a look in Charlie's eyes, bloodshot and stricken, like he was ready to cry, and Nelson thought at first that was a good sign, he thought surely Charlie would see the right thing to do now, but in one awkward motion he tumbled forward into both Sam and Roy, his fists pumping in wide arcs and his words coming out more like sobs. Roy spilled down rubber-legged to the floor and Sam stumbled back and then the two big men toppled onto the floor together, Charlie on top with his fists still flailing, Sam struggling underneath and now Melinda was out in the room yelling stop it, stop it, stop it, but Charlie wouldn't stop. Sam stretched face down on the floor now, the fists pounding the back of his head again and again, loud and sickening thumps that Nelson knew were never meant to be made between men, again and again, and Melinda scrambled down onto Charlie's back but he only shrugged her away, like a grizzly bear tossing off some little puppy, and he kept on hitting and Sam's legs lay still on the floor.

It was going where it shouldn't go now and No you don't, Nelson cried out. None of them knew what could happen like he did and he had to run in and stop it, there was nothing else to do, so he ran in and grabbed at Charlie's arm, telling him, Charlie don't do it, don't do it, but Charlie's elbow cocked back and smashed his cheek and he fell back hard on the floor. Charlie stopped then, his fist poised in the air, and he looked back to where Nelson sprawled, a look of confusion edging out the anger on his face.

That's enough, Charlie, Roy said, pulling himself up. He coughed and coughed and Get off him, he's knocked out cold, and he pulled at Charlie's shoulder.

You don't want to put him in a coma for Christsakes. Charlie raised up, his legs unsteady beneath him, his chest heaving for breath and his face red and swollen. I wasn't gonna let him choke you, he said, that's one thing for sure.

Melinda was on her knees and What's the matter with you? she said, looking up at both Charlie and Roy, the red tear tracks down her face. What did you do it for? and Roy only picked his cap up from the floor and dusted it off. Where's he got his money hid? he said looking down. That's all we came for, to get what's due us.

She didn't answer him but leaned over her father's wrecked shoulder whispering, Are you all right, are you all right? but he never moved, and Shit, Roy said to Charlie, see what you did, he's not gonna tell us anything now, and for a second Nelson's eyes connected with Charlie's and the regret over everything and how it was passed between them.

Now look, Melinda, Roy said. You might as well tell us where he keeps it at. I know you're the only one he'd tell, so you might as well just say where it is and we can get this whole deal over with.

All right then. All right. It's down behind the dome, she said, never looking up. That old geodesic dome by the pond. There's a rusted-out oil drum and it's buried under there. Now just get out of here. Get out of here and don't ever come back.

If I get what I came for, Roy said, I won't ever need to come back.

Wesley said Sam wasn't anything like Roy and Donna told him it didn't matter, people still went to prison for selling marijuana. The pen down at McAlester was full of young guys like that and what would Nelson think to have the big brother he always looked up to locked up like someone who wasn't fit to live with society?

I'm not going to prison or anywhere else, Wesley said. I'm just saying Sam Casey isn't like Roy.

I'm not going to argue with you, she said and drove on in silence, her mouth set firm and her eyes fixed on the road ahead. Driving felt awkward after so long a time, just keeping straight in the lane, turning the corners on the slick street, the hard shudder of the steering wheel in her grip. She concentrated on all of her movements in an exaggerated way and thought to herself the identities of things to keep her mind focused on what she was doing, a stop sign and a fire hydrant, an oak and a sycamore. A sparrow on the telephone wire, an old man with a shovel on his driveway, a plastic flamingo standing on one leg in a garden of snow.

He always said good things about you, Wesley said.

She looked at him. He stared through the windshield and she looked back at the road, surprised at how it felt to know that Sam Casey had been talking about her. I'm not saying anything bad about him, she said. I'm not judging him at all. But it doesn't matter what he's like, something could still happen. That's the way the world works, things can go wrong like that when you're not expecting it.

I know how the world works, he said.

She started to tell him that he didn't act like he did but she didn't say anything. Instead she concentrated on the snow coming down and the sliver of road ahead and the way the rolling tires sounded. They were outside of town now and the bar ditches were filling with snow and the bare trees specked the undulating hills like the bones of scarecrows gathered in lines and she wondered what it was exactly that Sam Casey had said about her and what Wesley had said in return. And Sam might have really meant it when he told her he was changing over to some new kind of business. Maybe he wanted to change more than anything else. Maybe he did. But wanting it was the easy part.

Roy hadn't been down to the geodesic dome in a long time. Ansel had built it over twenty years ago when he was going to be like Thoreau, live by the pond and find himself in nature and nature in himself. Or something like that. It had made sense to Roy at the time but it only seemed like foolishness now.

No trail led back that way anymore, only a field full of snow stretching to the tree line and the only marker was the metal gate in the rusted wire fence. Roy parked the truck in front of it, grabbed his six-pack up and told Charlie to get the shovel out of the back. In among the trees Roy walked toward where he thought the pond would be and behind him, lumbering noisily in the snow and brittle grass, Charlie said, Sam's probably all right, don't you think? I mean, Sam's probably all right, I don't think he's hurt all that bad, do you?

I don't know, Roy said, and to tell you the truth I don't care that much one way or the other. I'm through with that sonofabitch anyway.

Don't say that now.

You know what pisses me off more than any-thing? Roy said. He kept walking and never looked back. The way he said I did that jail time just so I could hang it over his head. Motherfucker. That's just like him to say shit like that.

I think we oughta go back there and see how he is, Charlie said.

You think anyone's gonna take a year in county just to hang it over somebody's head? Roy asked. I never did it for that. I mean, you wouldn't turn me in, would you, Charlie?

Hell no.

That's right, because you don't turn in family.

Real family, not like that sorry asshole old man of mine. You know? Sorry asshole like that and my mother just standing back and watching it. I'm not talking about that shit. I'm talking about real family. But then I get out of the fucking can and the thing was they treated me like some kind of fuckup stepchild. Sam and Ansel both. They always acted like I was just someone they had to put up with. Fuck that. That's all I have to say about that shit now. Fuck that.

Roy finished off what was left of his beer, threw the empty bottle into the snow, and pulled a full one from the six-pack. The crunching of the frozen grass filled the woods and the snow kept falling and finally he saw an opening ahead. The ten-foot-tall cedar dome sat out in the middle, the walls splintered and gray from the time gone by, dried grass grown up high around the bottom. The pond was frozen and all around the snow was perfect.

Roy stopped. Where's the damn oil drum?

What oil drum? Charlie stepped up beside him.

She said he had his money buried out here under a oil drum. Roy walked around the small wooden dome and by the edge of the pond. There isn't any fucking oil drum out here.

That's okay, Charlie said. I don't want any of that money anyway. I just want to keep working with him the way we been doing.

Fuck, Roy said. He dropped the six-pack in the

snow beside him, reared back and heaved his open bottle into the side of the dome. Fuck.

Come on, let's just go on back, Charlie said. He stood half-turned toward the woods, the shovel leaned across his shoulder.

Wait a minute. Wait just a minute now. Roy walked toward the pond. A rusty metal trash can lay decaying in the high grass a few feet away, holes eaten in the side and yellow stems of grass growing through. Maybe this is what she was talking about, he said. It looks like an old trash can some dogs or some coyotes or something got ahold of and drug off over here. Come here and bring that shovel.

I don't know, Charlie said. There's no telling where that can used to be.

Hey, we'll dig up the whole fucking place if we have to.

That's an awful lot of digging to have to go and do.

Well, shit, give me that thing then. Roy grabbed the shovel out of Charlie's hand. If you're so worried about Sam, go the hell on back up there then. I'll dig the shit up myself.

I just think we ought to go check on him, that's all, see if he's okay and everything.

You think he wants to see your ass back up there after what you did to him? Hell, he'll probably call the cops on you if you go back up there.

Sam wouldn't call the cops, he wouldn't do anything like that.

Roy squared around and jammed the blade of the shovel into the ground at his side. Fucking go on up there then. Take his side in the damn thing if you want to.

Charlie's eyes narrowed down and he looked almost ready to cry. I'm not taking anyone's side.

Go on, Roy said. Get the hell outta here. I got work to do. Go on now, you'll just get in my way anyway. He turned back, set his foot to the shovel and dug into the frozen earth. Only a small sliver, along with a layer of snow, came up, but he dug down again and again, keeping his eyes to the ground, furiously struggling with the metal blade, tearing at the hard-packed dirt, until the hole was more than a foot deep and then he stopped and, breathing hard, he looked up and Charlie was gone. The snow fell around him and down into the trees and he turned back to the ground, his eyes burning and a shaking inside he could barely contain.

When they got to the farmhouse, Donna parked behind Sam Casey's truck and told Wesley to just wait in the car, she would go up and get Nelson and that was all and they would go on home then. Wesley said he needed to take Melinda back but she said Sam Casey could do that.

She stepped out of the car and looked at the way the house sat back on the snow, the lights on in the windows, the green shutters and the tree in front, and then suddenly the door burst open and Nelson running toward her, hollering, his face red and tears on his cheeks and it was about Sam and Roy and Charlie and Sam being hurt.

Slow down, she said when he got to her but he grabbed onto her arm and nearly out of breath told her to come on, he might be hurt bad, pulling her on as he started back away.

Inside, the room was cold from the door being open and shadows reached out from all the corners. Sam Casey lay still on the floor, his daughter kneeling beside him, propping a pillow under his head, and blood on her hands and down on the knee of her pants. Blood on her hands and on the pillow and then for a second the smell of gunpowder again in the air, the ring of the shot, the car screeching away down the street, and the blood and the floor shifting beneath her. She turned and Wesley and Nelson stood behind her. The gray sky outside the front door and the snow falling down and her two boys, and Nelson said, We have to do something, and she said, We will.

She turned back and knelt by the girl and asked her what happened and she said it was a fight and Charlie had gone crazy and then the words got caught inside and Donna said, Do you have any alcohol?

We're going to need some if you have any. Or some Mercurochrome.

Melinda nodded and looked at her father. He was awake a second ago but he slipped off again, she said as she raised up. His forehead got cut on the floor and I've been trying to keep his head propped up. She gestured with her hands to show how she had done it and then moved away, her footsteps soft on the wood floor as she walked toward the kitchen. Donna looked at him then and he was pale, even his lips, a deep half-moon cut arching over his eyebrow, the blood leaking across the side of his face and a line of blood down from his swollen nose, and then his eyes flittered open and she started back. His head started to rise and his lips parted and her hands moved down to him, one cradling behind his head and the other on his shoulder.

Are you all right? she asked and he moved his mouth silently as though trying to remember how to talk and then he could only say, Help me get up, and his hand closed tightly around her arm.

You don't need to get up, she said. You just lay back down there and let me wash off those cuts. She helped him guide his head back to the pillow and then she felt another cut on the back of his head and the blood matted in his hair. She closed her eyes for a second and his grip was tight on her arm and then Melinda beside her saying, There wasn't any regular alcohol but I found this.

Donna took the open whiskey bottle and the smell of it rose up like the only atmosphere in the room. It's okay, she said, holding the bottle away from her face and forcing a calmness into her voice. He's awake now. He's all right.

Melinda handed her a washcloth and Donna poured the whiskey into it and began washing the cut above his eye and he winced and then opened his eyes again. Damn, he said. Don't tell me you're gonna try to kill me now.

Melinda and Nelson laughed from relief then and he smiled. She washed off the cuts and when she was finished he felt stronger and she and Wesley helped him onto the sofa. He held the washcloth to his forehead and she asked did he want to try taking some of the whiskey internally now and he told her she must have read his mind.

We'll have to take you over and get you some stitches, she told him and he took a pull on the whiskey and told her he guessed she was right about that but he figured he needed to sit down for a little bit longer.

When he was finally ready to try standing she told Wesley to go get the car started and turn on the heater. Sam was only a little unsteady on his feet but she held him around the waist and he rested his arms on her shoulders on the one side and Melinda's on the other. The porch steps were slippery from the snow and they held on tighter as they went down. He said the cold air felt good on his face. Look at that white field stretching down to the trees down there, he said. God, this place is beautiful sometimes.

The clouds bore down and the twisting limbs grew darker and no light overhead, not even some early star. The ground around the dome was pockmarked with the holes Roy had dug, all of them filling up with snow, and he said, Fuck it, and threw down the shovel. It wasn't over, he told himself, no, it still wasn't over, but he was too worn out to do anything more about it now.

At the edge of the woods, Charlie's footprints were fading in the snow but they didn't lead back to the truck. Instead they trailed into the trees and disappeared in the high grass, and Aw hell, Roy said. Charlie. Hey, you went the wrong damn way. No answer came and he walked on into the grass and trees and beyond that lay a gray bank of snow and black ice and a creek curving into twilight, nothing but jumbled whispers all around in the grass and the water, and Roy said, Fuck him if he thinks I care whether he went and got himself lost. They can all go to hell as far as I'm concerned, but he kept walking into the woods, a beer in one hand and the remnants of the six-pack swinging from the other.

At the side of the creek he thought he saw a dark figure under the ice but when he knelt down he couldn't

see through any better and it couldn't have been a person anyway. No one could live sealed under there like
that with nothing but the cold all around, and he stared
off into the trees. Charlie, he called out again. Where
the hell are you, goddamn it. I can't find any kind of
fucking path down here, and nobody called back and
the sheet of ice on the creek was blank.

He walked away from the creek and on through
the woods, up the long hill and then down and the
trees were even thicker and the snow falling and
another hill and at the top there was nothing but the
tangled branches and the white slope, no house or
structure of any kind, not even a telephone line loop-
ing down, and he waited for a long time, but there was
nothing else to do, and he started into the valley where
the snow gathered and the wind blew down any way
he turned.

In the car the heater blew hard toward the floorboard
and the heat rose up around them. Melinda sat in the
backseat with her father and Nelson sat between Wesley
and his mother, her arm wrapped around his shoulder.
The rolling banks at the side of the road were rounded
with snow and the fence posts and barbed wire and the
limbs of the trees struck against the white world. She
turned the radio on and it was nothing but an ad for a
used car lot, then static and then the ringing guitar
and I Want to Hold Your Hand, and out in the woods

269

nothing moved. It was like they were the only ones in the world but Nelson knew better than that. Roy Dale was out there and Ragel was in Texas and all the people and things he couldn't even see lay waiting in between.

In the backseat, Melinda told how she had made up the story about the buried money and she wondered if Roy was still down by the pond looking for it.

Probably not for long, Sam said. He'll be back, maybe not any more today but he'll be back eventually. It'd probably be best after I got these stitches if I went ahead and found him and had a talk with him and tried to get things ironed out before he gets up to anything else.

Nobody said anything. There was nothing but the radio and the sound of the heater and the tires in the snow. Then Sam said, I've known him too long.

Nelson felt his mother move against him then and she said, You don't have any business doing anything but laying down when you get back. You try driving out in this snow like this and you're liable to pass out cold.

I can drive him if he needs me to, Wesley said and Nelson watched her face against the window and the darkening sky, the straight line of her mouth, her serious eyes, and he waited for her to say something but she didn't. She never said anything, so he looked back and told Sam that he guessed he'd better go too then.

Her arm tightened around him and she started to

say something now but Sam leaned forward and said, That's all right, Nelson, I think you already helped me enough today.

That's right, she said. You've already done plenty, her fingers stroking down the side of his face and he'd forgotten how that could be.

Another old song came on the radio, the one about wild wild horses, and she turned up the volume. They started onto another road where no traffic had marked the white powder, the black trees gathered close on either side, the headlights cutting a path into the falling dark, and the sound of the radio and the heater and the tires in the snow.

A Reading Group Guide to
Falling Dark

Questions for Discussion

1. Is Donna a good mother?

2. Do you think the author, who is male, understands women? How about children? Why or why not?

3. The author gives us Nelson's rich fantasy life in quite a bit of detail. Why? In what ways does this help us to understand Nelson?

4. Both Donna and Wesley are capable of being fooled in love. Are the similarities in their susceptibility merely coincidental, or is there a deeper connection? Is it fair to say that they are simply dupes, or do they possess otherwise-valuable qualities that make them vulnerable?

5. Melinda and Jennifer have a complex friendship. On what is it built? What do they provide one another? In your opinion, is this a relationship that will last? What about other relationships in the book—Nelson and Ragel's, Donna and Sam's, Roy and Charlie's—what draws these people together? What

are the "healthiest" relationships in this novel, and how do we judge?

6. Sam Casey and the Sunshine People represent a certain brand of sixties idealism. Are there other kinds of idealists in this novel? In general, what do you think the book's attitude is toward idealistic philosophies?

7. Roy Dale is the obvious villain of the book. Do you ever get a sense of him as a human character, or is he more of a prop to keep the story moving along? If you sensed some depth to Roy's character, where in the book did you get the glimpses? Do you think it's more difficult to write believable "evil" characters than "good" ones, or the other way around? Why?

8. Are Roy's stories about raising Arabian horses and running a home for children pure, malicious bunk intended only as manipulation, or do you think they once were legitimate dreams of his? Does it make a difference?

9. Do you think the characters in this book are able to shape their lives and themselves through the choices they make, or do larger forces operate on them? What role does chance play? Guilt? Will? Forgiveness?

10. Is race important in this book? If so, in what ways?

11. Beyond small-town Oklahoma, the setting of the story isn't specified. Does this mean that the particulars of place aren't important here? Could this story have happened anywhere in America?

12. What does the title of the book mean to you? How is it important, or unimportant, to your understanding of the novel?

13. What do you think the major themes of the novel are? How do you see those themes dramatized?

14. Tim Tharp, like several other past and contemporary novelists, omits quotation marks around his dialogue. Why leave out something as standard as quotation marks? What effect did this have on you as a reader?

15. How do you feel about the way the novel concludes? Are all of your questions answered, or do you still have some? What do you foresee for these characters?

16. If you could ask the author one question about the book or about life, what would it be? What sort of answer would you expect?

About the Author

Tim Tharp was born in Henryetta, Oklahoma, and grew up in Midwest City, a suburb of Oklahoma City, where he discovered an interest in fiction writing as a fifth grader. After attending Oklahoma State University for two years, he left to explore the U.S., first by thumb and then in a battered pickup truck. Upon returning, he experimented with a variety of jobs, including factory hand, record store clerk, and psychiatric aid. In his late twenties, Tharp returned to college, earning a B.A. from the University of Oklahoma and an M.F.A. from Brown University. He currently teaches in the communications department at Oklahoma State University-Okmulgee. *Falling Dark* is his first published novel.

More Books for Reading Groups from Milkweed Editions

To make our books more valuable for reading discussion groups, we're pleased to offer guides to the following books free of charge on our website: www.milkweed.org. Please also check the site for guides added since this book's publication.

Aquaboogie by Susan Straight
A Keeper of Sheep by William Carpenter
The Children Bob Moses Led by William Heath
Cracking India by Bapsi Sidhwa
The Empress of One by Faith Sullivan
Homestead by Annick Smith
Persistent Rumours by Lee Langley
Seasons of Sun and Rain by Marjorie Dorner
The Tree of Red Stars by Tessa Bridal
Welcome to Your Life: Writings for the Heart of Young America
    edited by David Haynes and Julie Landsman

More Fiction from Milkweed Editions

To order books or for more information, contact Milkweed at
(800) 520-6455 or visit our website (www.milkweed.org).

Agassiz
Sandra Birdsell

My Lord Bag of Rice:
New and Selected Stories
Carol Bly

The Tree of Red Stars
Tessa Bridal

The Clay That Breathes
Catherine Browder

A Keeper of Sheep
William Carpenter

Seasons of Sun and Rain
Marjorie Dorner

Winter Roads, Summer Fields
Marjorie Dorner

Blue Taxis
Eileen Drew

Trip Sheets
Ellen Hawley

All American Dream Dolls
David Haynes

Live at Five
David Haynes

Somebody Else's Mama
David Haynes

The Children Bob Moses Led
William Heath

Pu-239 and Other Russian Fantasies
Ken Kalfus

Thirst
Ken Kalfus

Persistent Rumours
Lee Langley

Hunting Down Home
Jean McNeil

Swimming in the Congo
Margaret Meyers

Tokens of Grace
Sheila O'Connor

Tivolem
Victor Rangel-Ribeiro

The Boy Without a Flag
Abraham Rodriguez Jr.

Confidence of the Heart
David Schweidel

An American Brat
Bapsi Sidhwa

Cracking India
Bapsi Sidhwa

The Crow Eaters
Bapsi Sidhwa

Interior design by Anja Welsh and Karin Simoneau
Typeset in Janson
by Stanton Publication Services, Inc.
Printed on acid-free 55# Sebago Antique Cream paper
by Maple-Vail Book Manufacturing